DATE DUE

FE 17 '95	DE 4 '96		
MY 12 '95	RENEW		
JE 1 '95	AP 7 '97		
JY 6 '95			
MO 9 '95	MY 5 '97		
FE 23 '96	MO 3 '97		
MR 29 '96	DE 19 '97		
MY 17 '96	AV 27 '99		
MY 30 '96	JY 14 '99		
RENEW	MR 2 '00		
JY 25 '96	DE 4 '01		
AG 1 '96	FE 7 '02		
SE 20 '96	MR 22 '02		
OC 11 '96			
NO 15 '96	MY 10 '02		
MY 20 '97	NO 22 '08		

DEMCO 38-296

CONQUER RESUME OBJECTIONS

CONQUER RESUME OBJECTIONS

Robert F. Wilson
and
Erik H. Rambusch

JOHN WILEY & SONS, INC.

New York ▪ Chichester ▪ Brisbane ▪ Toronto ▪ Singapore

In recognition of the importance of preserving what has been written, it is a policy of John Wiley & Sons, Inc., to have books of enduring value published in the United States printed on acid-free paper, and we exert our best efforts to that end.

Library of Congress Cataloging-in-Publication Data:

Wilson, Robert F.
   Conquer resume objections / by Robert F. Wilson and Erik H. Rambusch.
     p.   cm.
   Includes index.
   ISBN 0-471-58984-5. — ISBN 0-471-58983-7 (pbk.)
   1. Job hunting—United States. 2. Career changes—United States. 3. Resumes (Employment)   I. Rambusch, Erik H., 1941–   II. Title.
HF5382.75.U6W54   1994
650.14—dc20   93-33090

Printed in the United States of America

10 9 8 7 6 5 4 3 2 1

Introduction

Conquer Resume Objections and the companion book *Conquer Interview Objections* are about job search. More specifically, they deal with the job search challenge by recognizing the difficulty of finding and keeping jobs in a time of profound change in the American marketplace. Such change may well have affected you personally, including as it has the permanent loss of hundreds of thousands of jobs (a magnitude unmatched since the Industrial Revolution). Since 1980, nearly 5 million men and women have lost jobs in *Fortune* 500 companies alone. An additional 300,000 military and civilian workers were "excessed" in the dozens of military bases closed around the country in the early 1990s. A cold war of four decades had the last laugh after all.

The challenge for job seekers from now till the end of the century and beyond resembles a game of musical chairs: workers eliminated from the employment "game," slowly but surely, as the number of job opportunities disappears, slowly but surely. Even when job loss levels off, the challenge will continue to be great because there will be much more competition for the remaining open jobs and new ones being created than there was a decade or more ago.

This is where *Conquer Resume Objections* comes in. Conventional job search methods won't—by themselves—assure success any more. All job seekers need an edge—strategies or work ways that propel them beyond their competitors—at every stage along the job-search continuum.

Your competition for any given job can be one person or a thousand—or somewhere in between. These two companion books offer a thorough, assertive game plan for making sure your candidacy stands out from that of others after the same job who believe that conventional job search is enough—or who don't know better.

The titles of the two books, *Conquer Resume Objections* and *Conquer Interview Objections*, are organized around two major areas of the job search. But look at the complete tables of contents for both books. You'll see every area of job search covered, from the day you decide to leave a job (or it decides to leave you) to the first weeks and months on your new job strategizing the rest of your professional life—and the best way to negotiate your first raise.

This volume, *Conquer Resume Objections*, is organized to help you:

1. Focus your search by addressing your specific situation, and shoring up weak spots in your candidacy—not only identifying them, but doing something about them

2. Organize your life—both professionally and personally—in the days and months ahead

3. Write the "flexible resume," a way of matching your resume with any job that comes along—by adjusting emphasis and focus where you need to

4. Develop an effective marketing plan that leaves nothing to chance

5. Overcome resume objections by anticipating what might sabotage your candidacy and taking any corrective action indicated.

If you have problems or questions further into the job search process, such as implementing your marketing plan, mastering the interviewing process, negotiating compensation, or finding the best ways to flourish on your next job, you'll want to take a look at *Conquer Interview Objections*.

PRONOUN/ADJECTIVE GENDER ALERT

Throughout this book our contribution to controlling the rampant use of "his or her," "his/her," "s/he," and "he/she," as well as various single subject-plural pronoun combinations, has been to generally characterize *job seekers* as male and *employers* as female. This is neither an ideal nor permanent solution, but the best we could think of. We're open to suggestions for improvement.

Acknowledgments

A number of friends and colleagues have contributed to the quality of this manuscript, among them Martha Buchanan, Mike Hamilton, Maureen Drexel, Nancy Jo Geiger, Jack H. Fuller, Charles Bove, Jack Couch, Lance Barclay, Jan Linley, John Tarrant, Tom Widney, Chuck Wielgus, Dave Brinkerhoff, Blanche Parker, Ellen Fish, Fran Williams, and Karen Wilner.

Contents

CONQUER
RESUME
OBJECTIONS

1

Getting Out From Under

Those of you who have decided to pick up this book are likely to be in one of the following five predicaments:

1. You do not have a job.
2. You're about to lose your job.
3. You hate your job and want another one.
4. You're having a tough time getting your first "real" job.
5. You're returning to the job market after years away from it.

Much of the information on the following pages will be of interest to you regardless of which of these five situations most resembles yours. Even if the symptoms of your professional malady aren't observable today, you'll be able to recognize them when you see them. For this reason you may want to pay particular attention to the section or sections relating most closely to your problem area(s), and just skim those sections that are less relevant.

Your strategy for getting into a new or better job will vary considerably depending on your situation—but yes, there will be similarities. The exception will be for those of you so new to professional life that you haven't been able to develop and refine your own special approach. In this sense Chapter 1 will be a primer of what situations, decisions, and behaviors to avoid as you begin to log some real time in the world of work.

RECENT JOB LOSS

You may bear the responsibility for losing your job or you may not, depending upon a variety of circumstances. Either way, you'll want to examine what went wrong in order to minimize the chances of it happening again.

Victims of Downsizing

Why is finding and keeping a job more difficult today than it was a decade ago? Let's label the fallen dominoes one by one: an increasingly spongy national economy; a decline in the number of manufacturing industries, particularly some of those related to defense; shrinking corporate profits; consolidation by acquisition and merger; massive organizational change; frequent business failure.

Since 1980, these overlapping phenomena have brought about the elimination of some 4.3 million jobs in *Fortune* 500 companies alone. Many have been middle-management jobs slashed to control growing business losses by flattening corporate infrastructure. Others have been phased out of existence by the relentless advance of technology—not just until a particular industry rebounds from whatever malaise has paralyzed it, but gone forever.

Older workers have been affected out of proportion to the rest of the workforce, according to Bureau of Labor Statistics. From October 1991 to October 1992, for example, unemployment for workers aged 16 through 54 rose 4.4 percent, while the rate for workers 55 and over increased by 31.4 percent.

So for these and other reasons, more Americans are applying for fewer jobs, while many of the people who get these jobs are performing very different duties than they did 10 years ago—often for less money.

Another sea change during this period is the redefinition of the fundamental relationship between employer and employee. Lifetime company tenure, common a generation ago, is virtually unknown today. Similarly, "company loyalty"—sometimes confused with family loyalty by those employers who have tended to blur the distinction—is in profound obsolescence. More and more frequently, once-faithful employees, some of whom have toiled 20 years or more in expectation of pension-augmented retirement, have been repaid with termination. Corporate "turnaround experts," paid big bucks to staunch the flow of red ink, usually find the solution in—aha!—bloated payrolls and loss-prone "profit centers."

Complicating this situation is a growing tendency among larger companies to "reengineer themselves," according to business behavior guru Peter Drucker. One manifestation of this, says Drucker in *Post-Capitalist Society*, is to rely on outside sources for some cyclical kinds of work, and in so doing eliminate entire layers of management and professional staff. "Most large companies have cut the number of layers by 50%, even in Japan," he said in a *Harvard Business Review* interview about the book. "Toyota came down from 20-odd to 11. GM has streamlined from 28 to maybe 19, and even that number is decreasing. Organizations will become flatter and flatter."

All of this will cause many job seekers to adopt a wary demeanor—and justifiably so. Guarding against the repeat of a possible downsizing squeeze, in particular, can approach the odds of a novice in a high stakes card game. Mix equal parts of luck and whimsy with sophisticated economic theory, and your guess will be as authoritative as the most seasoned economists' well-publicized forecasts.

For specific suggestions on ways to check out target companies later in your search that could lead you into the consequences of another reorganization or downsizing, see Chapter 4. For tips on interviewing with such companies, see Chapter 3 of *Conquer Interview Objections*, the companion to this book.

Termination "for cause"

Let's say you were partly, mostly, or wholly at fault for losing your last job. Your first priorities, of course, are to take care of such immediate needs as filing for unemployment compensation, determining your short- and long-term financial needs, and getting organized for the task ahead of you—all covered in Chapter 2.

Beyond this you need to *find out what to change about you or your next job* that may have contributed to the loss of your previous job. There may even be a reason to consider what to change about the way you *choose* jobs that could be getting in the way of professional success.

You may never have been told the real reason you were let go. Few firing authorities have the stomach to confront terminees about their major flaws. Many are just embarrassed to be in this position in the first place, or don't want to hurt people's feelings. Still others find firing such a painful act that they give the affected employee any reason for termination that will cause the least pain—both to themselves and to the person leaving.

Finally, an employer who discharges you in violation of any one of a number of federal and state statutes protecting workers, or who (in the language of the law) "otherwise discriminates against you," will go to considerable lengths to conceal any incriminating evidence. If you strongly believe that your employer has violated your rights based on any of the groups of laws listed below (adapted from Lewin Joel's comprehensive *Every Employee's Guide to the Law*), you may have cause for retributive action:

- Civil rights laws protecting you from discrimination based on your age, sex, race, religion, ethnic background, or handicap

- Constitutional First Amendment laws granting you freedom of speech, freedom of religion, freedom of the press, and freedom of assembly (provided your activities did not interfere with your job performance or your working relationship with your employer)

- Laws that protect your right to engage in "concerted activity" (read picketing and strikes) or belong to a union

- Wage and hour laws that guarantee the minimum wage you must be paid (with exceptions for trainees, volunteers, and workers who depend on tips in addition to their paychecks)

- Laws designed to protect your safety and health, chiefly the Occupational Safety and Health Act of 1970 (OSHA)

- Equal pay laws (for men and women)

- Laws that protect your personal privacy, and access to personnel records your company kept on you (varies widely by state)

- Laws that prohibit discharge or discipline because your wages have been attached by a creditor[1]

This is not to say that you should go out of your way to lash back at an employer for spite, on the mistaken notion that "getting even" will somehow atone for any wrong that has been done you.

---

[1] Joel, *Every Employee's Guide to the Law*.

If your grievance is whimsical and without merit, not only will your efforts fail, but your reputation as a "troublemaker" will precede you and adversely affect your ability to get future jobs.

Getting a Second Opinion

Firsthand information about your previous situation is invaluable. A former co-worker, for example, can provide information you never had or give you a level of detachment and objectivity you are unable to reach on your own—in some instances, both.

Choose your sources carefully. The last thing you want to do is reinforce a misimpression or add tainted new information to the mix. A former colleague at your level or above is more likely to give you an accurate and honest evaluation of your situation than someone at a level or more lower than the job you held. Former direct reports are the least reliable sources of all because they may view themselves on the wrong end of a "blamed messenger" situation, and either equivocate or withhold information accordingly.

Another caveat: Some of your contacts may feel an obligation to say only good things about the company or your ex-boss. After all, they still have their jobs, and you don't. Encourage candor by assuring them that your sole purpose for calling is to learn about yourself and apply what you learn to your next job.

Contact three or four people with whom you worked closely and enjoyed a good professional relationship. Evening calls at home are best, because you'll probably catch your source person at a more relaxed time—and with more privacy—than you will at the office. If you do have to call at work for whatever reason, pick your times carefully. If you know your source is an early arriver, for example, call before 9:00 A.M. If he lunches late, call after noon. If he normally works late, call after 5:00 P.M.

For this person to be of maximum value, you need to encourage complete honesty and candor at the outset. Here is a model you can adapt for your own purposes and style:

"Hello, Rich? This is Bart Nelson. Is this a good time to talk for a few minutes? Good. I wanted to ask you a question that might be difficult for you to answer, but I really need you to level with me.

"I've been doing a lot of thinking since I left Ajax, as you might imagine, and I don't want what happened there to happen at my next job—even if it means a career change.

"Here's how you can help me, Rich, if you will. I want you to think back on any ways I could have improved my performance [work habits; personal relationships] that might have prevented me from having to leave.

"Don't feel you have to give me an answer right now. . . . Take a day or two if you'd like, and I'll get back to you at whatever time is good for you. The important thing is for you to be brutally honest with me. Sugarcoating is not going to help me at this point, so please let the chips fall where they may. I can take it, and I really need some straight answers—for my own sake."

Other questions that may be useful for you to ask are:

"In general, what do you think my co-workers thought of me?"

"How do you think I could have improved my relationships with a) my boss; b) my peers; c) my subordinates?"

"How do you think I could have improved my performance at Ajax?"

"What did you see as my strong points?"

"What do you think was the biggest thing that went wrong for me at Ajax?"

"Is that why you think I was let go?" (If not—or if there were other contributing factors—probe for additional answers.)

"If you were me, what would you do differently on the next job?"

Write all of these questions down with enough space after each so you can record the responses. If you're not sure that you got a complete answer, ask your source to repeat it and elaborate, if necessary.

This is risky business, obviously. Having put yourself on the line like this, you need to mean it when you say you want complete candor and not get defensive if one of Rich's responses hurts your feelings or makes you angry. Just keep in mind that: (1) Every negative thing you learn about yourself can be used for your own good; (2) any pain you suffer from these calls will be temporary— and ultimately beneficial; and (3) the next person you talk with may have an overwhelmingly positive comment about working with you that will "make your day."

Speaking of "the next person," it is important that you not rely on just one source to determine what went wrong. Try to reach and process the comments of at least three people to optimize the accuracy of the opinions you solicit. Synthesize all of the answers from this raw data to help you in planning a course of action. The following outline should help you organize each of your feedback discussions, as well as analyze what you learn from them.

JOB-RELATED STRENGTHS

Skills and Knowledge	Interpersonal Tactics

AREAS FOR IMPROVEMENT

Skills and Knowledge	Interpersonal Tactics

Your investigations, plus any additional insight you can provide, should light the way for a career decision—even if it is based on significant negative feedback and indicates a career path you should *not* pursue. Following are several common categories of work dissatisfaction that may have contributed to your dismissal or your quitting. If you see yourself in any of them, it may well be time to consider corrective action.

Burnout

Burnout has been part of the workplace vocabulary for less than 20 years, first having been used in the late 1970s to define "mental fatigue from job tedium and stress." Nevertheless, although it still isn't listed in some dictionaries, burnout probably is close to the top of the dozen or so most frequently heard maladies describing job dissatisfaction.

In 1986 a University of Georgia study of 33 public- and private-sector organizations reported that 45 percent of all employees suffer from psychological burnout to some extent. At greatest risk are those workers who hold jobs with ambiguous descriptions and receive little supervisory support, but who are still under high pressure to produce.

According to the Georgia study, here are some classic symptoms of burnout:

- Indifference to assignments, deadlines, and workload
- Impatience with family and friends
- Increased use of alcohol, food, or drugs
- Persistent fantasies about "running away"
- Overwhelming feelings of inadequacy about both work and personal life.

If you see that one or more of these symptoms can be applied to you during the last weeks or months of a job you lost, burnout may have been your problem—or at least one of your problems. Such manifestations of emotional exhaustion have for some time been identified with a number of the "helping professions," among them police officers, fire fighters, counselors, teachers, nurses, social workers, psychiatrists, physicians, psychologists, and attorneys (not to mention those human resource professionals responsible for administering the layoffs and downsizing mentioned earlier).

For those workers whose professional commitment may reflect not only a considerable investment in time and money but also the fulfillment of a lifelong dream, career change may be out of the question. Family or personal obligations may preclude the kind of interruption that retraining of any duration may require. Nevertheless, a change of some kind is indicated—to salvage mental, emotional, and physical health.

With this in mind, be aware that there are certified career counselors in nearly every city to help you deal with your situation. However, also be aware that some counselors who put out shingles have little or no background, education, or training in the field. The premier agency governing them is the National Board of Certified Counselors, which has rigorous testing and educational standards, as well as a code of ethics, for those it certifies. Ask all prospective counselors for their credentials.

Corporate Misfit[2]

A corporate culture is a powerful force, impervious to individual pressure—or even group pressure—to change. Corporate norms affect an individual's attitude and performance from a number of different perspectives. They occur in such areas as information sharing (it either is a norm or it isn't), innovation (it's either encouraged or it isn't), self-expression, and socializing with one's work group.

Industrial psychologists have identified two basic types of corporate culture. In a "closed" corporate culture, as described in a study by Professor Ralph H. Kilmann of the University of Pittsburgh, work units guard their fiefdoms carefully and share little information. They protect themselves at all times, minimizing risks and generally exhibiting extreme caution. An "adaptive" corporate culture, on the other hand, requires both risk and trust. Employees actively support one another's efforts to identify problems and reach solutions.

Individuals who don't tune in quickly to the many nuances of their corporation's culture usually find themselves in deep trouble.

---

[2]The next few "misfit" sections are adapted from *Job-Bridge*, a corporate outplacement program published by Wilson McLeran, Inc., New Haven, CT 06511. *Job-Bridge* uses the term "misfit" to connote an *inappropriate* job fit, and not to reflect on the abilities or character of any individual locked in a destructive working environment.

Those who are patient and clever enough to go through the motions can survive until they are able to find a position with another company in which the culture is more in tune with their own work habits, attitudes, or style. Mavericks who think they can buck or change the system, however, are in for a rough time. Without compromise, in fact, their paydays definitely are numbered.

Functional Misfit

If you have a problem identifying with the kind of work you are doing, perhaps your functional fit is wrong. Maybe there is a misalignment between your responsibilities and the kinds of things you like to do in a work situation. (Later on there is an assessment tool that will help you find out for yourself.) For example, do people, data, or things dominate the work you have been doing? If your last job was as a computer programmer, for example, and more than anything else you like to work with people, you could be a functional misfit.

Don't conclude from this evidence alone that it is time to change careers, however. What you have is an *indicator*, not a mandate, which should at least cause you to investigate further, until the signals become clearer. Most jobs, in fact, involve working with people, data, *and* things, rather than any one of them to the exclusion of the other two.

To take your hunch further, spend some time in the library with the *Dictionary of Occupational Titles*, as well as any other suggestions your librarian can offer. The DOT, published by the U.S. Department of Labor, categorizes some 20,000 jobs on the basis of whether they are oriented more toward people, data, or things.

Much more comprehensive is John L. Holland's *The Self-Directed Search*, including his Occupations Finder. In one to three hours—and for $4.00—you can score yourself in six behavioral areas: Realistic, Investigative, Artistic, Social, Enterprising, and Conventional. The SDS is answered, scored, profiled, and interpreted by the user against the Occupations Finder, which provides descriptive codes for nearly 500 occupations.

If the results of the SDS are not conclusive, Dr. Holland and his associates have prepared a *Vocational Exploration and Insight Kit*. This handy tool takes the SDS a step further, but it must be administered by a professional counselor or psychologist. (Other assessment tools frequently used by counselors are discussed in "You're After Your First Full-time Job," on page 21.)

Industry Misfit

This should be the easiest of misfits to fix. If you find your job function satisfying, but the industry you're in distasteful, meaningless, alien, or boring, resuscitate your membership contacts in any functional professional societies—local, state, regional, or national.

Most functions travel quite well from industry to industry. Financial analysts, personnel directors, corporate attorneys, information systems managers, media relations specialists, and purchasing agents usually do equally as well in cosmetics as they do in sheet metal or natural gas. More often than not an industry switch is just a matter of improving one's network to find out where the action is.

Managerial Misfit

All managers must learn to train, delegate, mediate, motivate, influence, encourage, evaluate, correct, and change behavior—sometimes on the spot, and sometimes without benefit of training. When unforeseen problems surface, corrective action often has to be identified and administered immediately. The way a manager handles a sensitive employee's mistake can affect that person's performance—sometimes permanently.

In the face of such sizable responsibilities, it seems only logical that companies would spend considerable time and money training managers to be effective leaders. This happens less frequently than it should, sad to say, and most men and women promoted into supervisory positions are left to manage by either common sense or instinct. Some improve their skills after a few years on the job; others never improve at all. Read on to see if your problem might have been, or might still be—managerial.

David McClelland, a psychologist, and David Burnham, a management consultant, teamed to produce a study of managerial styles published in *Psychology Today* several years ago. Their research revealed three clear-cut approaches to management, based solely on the personalities and apparent psychological needs of the individuals tested. As you will see, the three styles offered starkly differing degrees of effectiveness, as follows:

Good-guy bosses. Managers with an overwhelming need to be liked (or who are extremely afraid of being disliked) tend to be lousy bosses. They believe that a happy ship is an effective ship, and that tight supervision only rocks it. Their directives and deadlines are usually vague, their criticism is rarely specific, and their response to unsatisfactory performance is often bumbling or inappropriate.

A good-guy boss often makes exceptions to company rules just to keep on good terms with employees to whom specific favors are granted. Consequently, such a boss frequently alienates those workers who are trying to go by the corporate book. They see their boss's inconsistent application of the rules as rendering them powerless to control their professional lives. Whether they perform well or poorly, they don't know what to expect next.

Because good-guy bosses care more about fellowship than effectiveness, they also have trouble giving critical feedback to subordinates. Fearing that they won't be liked if they give negative feedback, they either minimize it, don't offer it clearly and honestly, or don't give it at all.

McClelland and Burnham found that good guys ran fewer than 25 percent of all departments that performed "above average" under their criteria, and more than 75 percent of all departments that functioned "poorly."

Power-trip bosses. Managers who regard their departments or divisions as personal turf usually make good short-term bosses, but generally are ineffective over the long haul. Because they rule by fear and threat, they are indeed obeyed. And yes, deadlines and objectives are met.

McClelland and Burnham found, however, that most power-trip bosses want their subordinates to be loyal to *them*, personally, often at the expense of organizational goals. Because they reward only blindly faithful subordinates, however, their long-term effectiveness is markedly diminished. Power-trip bosses tend to have high turnover in their departments. Those who report directly to them and are not part of the "in group" are usually reluctant to offer ideas, knowing that they will rarely, if ever, get credit for them. Thus, innovation and improvement are seldom associated with power-trip bosses, unless they generate it themselves.

The middle road. If either of the two extremes described above bears even the faintest resemblance to a style of leadership that has caused you trouble in the past, this section may help you take corrective action.

Between the good-guy boss and the power-trip boss is room for a sizable gray area of management style that harnesses and redirects power—not for its own sake necessarily, but in a team effort toward the fulfillment of short- and long-term company objectives. McClelland and Burnham call such bosses "institutionalized-power managers."

They are also called by other researchers "assertive delegators"— as opposed to "nonassertive delegators" (good-guy bosses), and "aggressive delegators" (power-trip bosses).

In *The Way of the Ronin,* Beverly Potter describes the boss as a coach who operates under fairly stringent guidelines. (In feudal Japan, Ronin were samurai who left the service of their masters to make their own way in the world. With neither money nor transferable skills, they had to live by their wits. Potter uses the book's title as a metaphor for career strategies today.) Her five fundamental principles for this kind of successful leadership are summarized below:

1. *Tell the employee* what targets are to be reached and provide regular feedback to monitor, adjust, and redirect performance as necessary. Be concise, specific, and direct. Avoid vague guidelines ("We expect you to show initiative") and judgmental or emotional statements ("That was a half-assed job"). Describe no more than one situation at a time.

2. *Ask for information* in order to elicit participation and develop employee potential. Probe with open-ended questions ("What are you looking for?" is better than "Are you ready for responsibility?"). Avoid "why" questions which tend to put employees on the defensive. Ask enough questions to get all relevant information and communicate that you are listening seriously.

3. *Describe specifically* how the information and suggestions you gathered during the *Ask* stage will be translated into a plan of action. Indicate who will do what, under what conditions, and to what extent. Vaguely stated plans lead to problems of interpretation and accountability. Negotiate the plan with the employees. Draw upon their experience and knowledge, and encourage their commitment.

4. *Check performance frequently* so you'll be able to take quick action at the first sign of trouble. Monitor employees at different hours and in varying sequences to preclude peak performance only at check times. Use charts and graphs where possible to motivate performers at all levels. Encourage self-charting to allow employees to record and rate their own performances.

5. *Acknowledge and reinforce* good performance. Comment on specific actions. Tailor your positive feedback to the individual. Pay

attention to ways in which the person is performing as desired. Encourage employees to acknowledge and reinforce one another. Likewise, encourage self-acknowledgment, which is the cornerstone of high self-esteem, and is essential for self-starting and self-directing behavior.

Potter maintains that a Ronin management style will permit managers to get the most out of their creative and autonomous subordinates, and at the same time allow employees who lack self-direction to similarly contribute a peak performance.

Frederick G. Harmon, in *The Executive Odyssey*, adds a somewhat more subtle criterion for successful leadership. Though the executive's hours are dominated by physical and mental work, Harmon believes that "the single greatest work involved in career advancement is psychological effort, the below-the-surface, behind-the-scenes battle that individuals wage in restraining their ego, in working to improve the impact they have on others, and in shaping themselves to the requirements of the work."

Behavioral Misfit

Many people have trouble adjusting to group norms. Some just don't care how they come off, while others have no idea that their personalities are abrasive, disruptive, or alienating.

There are many gradations of behavior, ranging from completely acceptable to completely unacceptable. All behavior can be judged by myriad values and standards.

At one extreme are the mavericks, whose highly individualized way of looking at problems or life can be thwarted in a corporate culture that rewards lock-step behavior and punishes anything else. That's why many mavericks are marginal corporate misfits.

At the other extreme are those individuals who need psychological help, or whose behavior is otherwise influenced by domestic problems. These are situations that need attention, obviously, but are beyond the scope of this book.

The vast middle ground is where you likely will find yourself if you suspect that an attitudinal problem played a part in a recent dismissal. But unfortunately, as the deodorant commercial went years ago, "Even your best friends won't tell you."

Reread your notes from the former-colleague-feedback telephone calls (described on page 5) if you think your attitude may have contributed to any job problem you had.

As a way of consolidating what you have learned about yourself in the previous sections, complete the following fitness report, and guide yourself accordingly:

FITNESS QUOTIENT

	(Tightfit)								(Misfit)
	10	9	8	7	6	5	4	3	2	1

Corporate _____

Functional _____

Industry _____

Managerial _____

Behavioral _____

Scoring:

10–9	Tightfit; keep moving in this direction
8–7	Good Fit; must improve for long-term success
6–4	Marginal Fit; substantial change indicated
3–0	Misfit; get out as soon as you can

Getting a Handle on Your Preferences

Another way of assessing the plusses and minuses of your last (or current) position is to take an inventory of them. Spend a few minutes analyzing your feelings about the job you just left. This will help you decide the extent to which you should continue to pursue the kind of work you seem to favor. (If your pattern is to change jobs every couple of years or so, first find out why.)

Draw a vertical line down the middle of a piece of paper (or on your computer screen), with the left-hand side allocated for positive responses, the right-hand for negative. Base your responses on the sum of your experiences, drawing on all of the activities, skills, responsibilities, contacts with people, work conditions, and other factors that may have relevance. Here are several areas worth covering; you may well think of others:

What I Liked . . .   **What I Didn't Like . . .**

About the job:

_____

_____

_____

About the function
(the type of work, e.g., accounting):

_____

_____

_____

About the company:

_____

_____

_____

About the industry:

_____

_____

_____

Other:

_____

_____

_____

Then, using the responses you have written and any further thoughts you may have, complete the following statements:

At work I need: _____

_____

I am interested in: _____

_____

I excel at: _____

_____

I don't do well at: _____

I like to: _____

_____

I don't like to: _____

_____

I try to avoid: _____

_____

I value: _____

_____

Charles Bove, a Hamden, Connecticut, career consultant, adds to this list a request for the job seeker to describe "the ideal job," including responsibilities, advancement opportunities, salary level, benefits, location, size of organization, and the extent to which it is compatible with "your interests, aptitudes, and educational major."

The data generated by these exercises provide only half of the picture. You still need to know what to do with your information. If your path is still unclear after following the suggestions in this book, take your information and inclinations to a certified career counselor, such as Mr. Bove—one who can provide references of satisfied clients.

YOU HATE YOUR JOB ENOUGH TO QUIT

More than likely you've found on the previous pages of this chapter at least one of the reasons you want to leave your job, as well as a possible alternative that will help you extricate yourself. We've covered the most frequently heard job complaints—except possibly for the one about the brother-in-law who is also your boss, for which we have no suggestions that won't get you into further trouble.

Changing Careers

Engineering a sharper change, perhaps to a completely different career, will take longer to consummate—maybe years. If the job you want represents a dream of long standing, it will help to look at its pursuit almost as a hobby. First, acknowledge that reaching your goal will take time. This will help to keep your frustration in check. Second, allocate some spare hours every week researching and networking your next career. Become an expert, so that you will be *perceived* as an expert.

Even a small career change is a formidable undertaking, requiring considerable thought and preparation. Unless you have adequate financial resources to skip paychecks during the time it takes to retrain or go back to school, it is better to get a job like the one you just left, and work on your change part time until you can make the break without undue financial sacrifice.

Schools for Career Changers

A number of community colleges and smaller universities throughout the country provide programs that make it relatively painless for employed professionals to change careers. At some institutions students can complete a nationally accredited M.B.A. program, for example, by attending weekend classes over a two-year period. Others offer high school diplomas, two-year associate's degrees, or programs specially designed for career advancement or change. Let's look at two that may be typical of opportunities available in your area.

Olympic College is a public, state-supported, two-year college outside Seattle, Washington for high school grads, but that includes adult high school diploma and high school equivalency programs, as well. It offers three associate degrees (Arts and Sciences, General Studies, and Technical Arts), with a chance to apply business, industry, or government experience—for credit—toward the degree in technical arts. Study leads toward such diverse occupations as welding, retail fashion marketing, nursing, and real estate.

Concordia University, in River Forest, Illinois, offers a program for adult students (average age is 39.4 years) to earn a bachelor's degree in Organizational Management, rather than in a specific subject. Entry requirements to this private institution include two years of college for a degree enabling students to either advance more easily in their current careers, or change to one more in tune with today's marketplace.

"The competition for students is keen everywhere," says Continuing Education Dean Elaine Sipe. "The advantage for us has been our location, as well as the strong one-on-one attention we're able to offer students." The average student typically represents such industries as human resources, small business ownership, telecommunications, social work, and engineering. Call nearby colleges for possible similar opportunities.

Checking your "Negative Success Quotient." A frequently overlooked category of potential career changers are the many *successful* people profoundly unhappy in their jobs. According to Charles Bove, even salesmen exceeding their quota for three straight years and executives with enviable performance records come to him "with headaches, chest pains, unable to sleep, or exhausted—all wanting to get out of their particular bind, at any cost." The common denominator, says Bove, is the individual's body sending a message that something wrong needs correcting. "Sometimes a subtle change from sales to administrative management is enough. For others, only a more drastic change will trigger a sufficient enough boost in one's self-esteem, self-worth, and ability to feel good in general."

Finding a Job That Matches Your Personality

Before the headaches arrive, an alternative might be to make sure your personality fits the career path you've chosen. One of the instruments many career counselors and psychologists use is the Myers-Briggs Type Indicator test, which is designed to detect differences in personality types.

Developed by Katherine Briggs and her daughter, Isabel Myers, the MBTI has its roots in the work of psychologist Carl Jung, who discovered that people with different personalities also have vastly different ways of receiving and processing information. Jung classified people into four basic types in this regard: Sensing, Intuiting, Thinking, and Feeling.[3]

None of these classifications is related to intelligence, Jung said, nor is one necessarily better than the others. Here are a few ways to distinguish among the four that may help you determine why you don't like your job, as delineated in the executive newsletter *Working Smart*[4]:

---

[3]These four types surface again in the companion book, *Conquer Interview Objections*, as an aid in classifying job interviewers.

[4]*Working Smart*, © Learning International, Inc., 1985.

Sensing Types

- Excel at precision work
- Avoid learning new skills
- Come unglued when projects get too complicated
- Prize accuracy over originality
- Are slow to make decisions

Intuitive Types

- Grumble about routine duties
- Constantly seek new challenges
- Relish solving complex problems
- Frequently make errors of fact
- Reach quick, and often hasty, conclusions

Thinking Types

- Respond to logic, not emotion
- Need to be treated fairly
- Tend to be firm-minded
- Remain cool during office feuds
- Can reprimand or fire without flinching

Feeling Types

- Are sensitive to others' feelings
- Seek occasional praise
- Make decisions that take into account others' opinions and needs
- Are unnerved by confrontations
- Dislike criticizing others

In selecting a career, build on your strengths. Most Intuitives won't be happy in a job that requires extensive attention to detail, nor will most Thinkers shine in sales. We say "most" because this is, of course, only a general interpretation, not a full-fledged analysis.

More about making career change happen will be covered in later chapters.

YOU'RE AFTER YOUR FIRST FULL-TIME JOB

The distressing news continues for high school or college graduates seeking to make their way in the professional world. Even top graduates and newly minted Ph.D.s are having difficulty finding jobs, or even lining up interviews. Throughout the Ivy League, about half the June 1993 seniors needing a job didn't have one as of graduation.

Specialists in the humanities have experienced these difficulties for the past several years. Only recently, though, have scientists and mathematicians begun to suffer the same fate, many of them victims of the federal government's increasing lack of support for space and weapons programs.

The Incredible Shrinking Job Market

Many of these young people are facing the distressing prospect of changing careers without ever having experienced their original career choice. A painfully tight job market has forced some of these graduates to abandon their training in aerospace, for example, for less satisfying positions in the computer industry where some "crossover" possibilities exist. Others are going back to school for additional degrees that will give them more latitude in analogous fields, or will offer them teaching credentials.

Because entire books and programs have been written for those of you new to seeking full-time work (good ones, too—a couple of them are listed in the bibliography at the end of this chapter), this book and its companion probably will not be your only source. Most of these programs can complement the advice you will receive from the many competent college or high school guidance counselors trained to point you in the right direction.

Nevertheless, there are some fundamental decisions to make, foremost of which is what *you* want to do with the rest of your professional life, irrespective of marketplace needs. If all goes well, you have the best of everything: Your dream job is also work the marketplace wants done *now*, for big bucks—until you decide you want something else.

As noted above, however, it almost never happens this way. That's why the "ideal" is so frequently unattainable. But there are ways to get closer to your ideal than would have been possible had you not tried.

One way to begin is to think of subjects and activities you like and are good at, and that also match duties and responsibilities for various kinds of jobs you research. Interests and preferences are one part of the puzzle.

Apprenticeships for Your First Job

Those of you in college or on your way should know that most large corporations are hiring only those graduating seniors who have interned for them as undergrads. Says Bill Dittmore, director of recruitment and college relations for General Mills: "About a third of our offers to new grads go to people who already have worked for us as interns. We plan to raise that to between 40 percent and 50 percent."

Union Carbide and other corporations have also set 50 percent as their targeted minimum of intern hires. This puts the pressure squarely on freshmen and sophomores to get involved in their careers early for any chance at a job in a big company after graduation. And these days, to complicate matters, the competition comes not only from peers but from out-of-work adults.

The lion's share of future opportunities however, will lie beyond the *Fortune* 500 companies. This being so, the trick is to research smaller companies and inquire about internships—or summer jobs—where the field will be less crowded. And if the internship doesn't pay off, a resume that reveals not only good grades and career-related extracurriculars, but solid work experience as well, is the one that will stand out and get the interviews.

For those of you still unsure of your direction, contact a certified career counselor. Various assessment tools are available to them that measure interest levels, "career personality," intellect, and aptitude. Specific tips on writing the most effective resumes and cover letters for new job seekers can be found in Chapter 3.

GETTING BACK INTO THE JOB MARKET

Those of you who have been away from your career field for a year or more—raising children, or shoring up a family business in trouble, for example—face a stigma of another kind. The perception will be that you are "out of touch" with recent developments in your industry or function. Unless you've been away for five years or more and automation or another kind of accelerated technology has made your job very different from the way you remember it, the charge won't stick. Unfortunately, it's the *perception* that will do you in, and on that basis the decision not to take a chance on you will be made.

So your first obligation is to overcome the stigma by researching everything that went on in your industry or function during the time you were away; over-researching, actually, because you will be held to much more stringent scrutiny than will a candidate with skills and experience no stronger than yours, but without an employment gap to fight. If in your time away from the job you took on any volunteer or part-time consulting assignments that can be documented as career-related, be sure to take these into consideration.

Many such part-time assignments have led to full-time jobs. Think of them as steps that give you the opportunity to demonstrate your skills, your willingness to work, and the ability to build positive human relationships.

Although there are indications that parenting responsibilities are beginning to be shared more equally, this has not noticeably increased the number of men coming back to resume careers after full-time fatherhood duties. Many university and community college career centers specialize in assisting women returning to the marketplace, including counseling and testing services. Drop in on the one nearest you to find out what assistance is available.

More about tactical considerations will be presented as the discussion moves into other aspects of the job search later in this book and in its companion, *Conquer Interview Objections.*

ADDITIONAL READING

Bastress, Frances. *The Relocation Spouse's Guide to Employment.* Chevy Chase, MD: Woodley Publications, 1989. Fifty-one cases reveal how to conduct a job search as a "trailing spouse."

Bell, Arthur H. *International Careers.* Holbrook, MA: Bob Adams, Inc., 1990. Six steps for finding an international job. Reference section offers detailed information on U.S. firms that employ internationally, foreign employers, foreign embassies in the U.S., and temporary overseas opportunities.

Bird, Caroline. *Second Careers: New Ways to Work After 50*. Boston: Little, Brown, 1992. Analyzes the career switches of 6,347 people over 50 in nearly 300 occupations. Why they moved; what they learned; how they got their present jobs.

Campbell, David. *If You Don't Like Where You're Going, You'll Probably End Up Somewhere Else*. Allen, TX: Tabor Publishing, 1974. How to understand, appreciate, and utilize your assets. Good advice on making the most of what you have by the co-author of the Strong-Campbell Interest Inventory.

Crowther, Karmen N.T. *Researching Your Way to a Good Job*. New York: John Wiley & Sons, Inc., 1983. Provides tools and techniques to examine potential employers and jobs; job-related information on other communities if you intend to relocate.

Joel, Lewin G. *Every Employee's Guide to the Law*. New York: Pantheon Books, 1993. The front-cover blurb says it all: Everything you need to know about your rights in the workplace—and what to do if they are violated.

Keirsey, David, and Marilyn Bates. *Please Understand Me*. Del Mar, CA: Prometheus Nemesid Books, 1978. Explores a variety of character and temperament types, describing each in detail and enabling the reader to understand his own behavioral patterns and apply that insight to daily decisions.

Landau, Suzanne. *The Landau Strategy: How Working Women Win Top Jobs*. New York: C.N. Potter; distributed by Crown, 1980. Uses 17 cases to demonstrate target market definition, match tactics to interview types, salary negotiation strategy.

Munschauer, John L. *Jobs for English Majors and Other Smart People*. Princeton: Peterson's Guides, Inc., 1991. Literate job search companion for the liberal arts major. How to match wits with interviewers, create openings for oneself, learn how to use the language of employers.

Wilson, Robert F., and Janet Hollander. *Job-Bridge*. New Haven: Wilson McLeran, Inc., 1989. Award-winning career transition program used by corporations nationwide to assist terminated employees. Text, workbook, planner, and videotape. Sound advice for those faced with unexpected job search.

2

Getting Organized

One of the most difficult chores of a job search is to keep administratively organized and make the best use of your time. Time is an irretrievable resource; nevertheless, sound organization and time management do not necessarily mean cramming more and more scheduled activities into your day. They mean doing the right things properly—which actually might result in doing *less, more effectively*.

Some people who appear very disorganized accomplish a great deal. Looking more closely at the way they work often reveals good organizational skills packaged in terms of key activities.

Consider the "absent-minded professor." His lab is a mess; he doesn't know what day it is; his royalty checks remain in a dresser drawer, uncashed. All of this may simply mean that he has prioritized his time, and doesn't worry about many of the details that consume most of the rest of us.

After all, the professor does complete his experiments, and presumably writes his books to deadline. When his bills are piled high enough, he'll cash a few checks.

For those of you in job transition, unfortunately, matters usually seem somewhat more complicated. And for those of you used to the support services a secretary once provided, the job is tougher yet. For example, you'll need to work out ways to handle:

- Message-taking
- Telephone-answering
- Typing
- Proofreading
- Scheduling
- Researching

Those of you in more rarefied executive air may even have counted on others for assistance balancing your checkbook, running errands, and computing your expense account. For you, many of the topics in the rest of Chapter 2 may seem particularly difficult. Those who have completed successful job searches, however, agree that one of the hardest parts of the process was in managing the details. Tracking all of the messages, keeping on top of the correspondence, and remembering all of the names and circumstances of meetings with target company officials can become an overwhelming mass of seeming trivia. It is also essential to your success in finding the best possible next job.

Taking on all of these responsibilities yourself in an effective manner requires time and resources management in three areas: (1) managing finances; (2) organizing your office; and (3) organizing your day.

FINANCIAL MANAGEMENT

If you are out of a job, your sense of urgency will be stronger than if you are drawing regular paychecks, no matter how meager. Now is the time to take stock of your finances and make the decisions that will allow you enough time and peace of mind to conduct your job search in a rational, effective manner. Undue worry about your financial status can lead to panic, which in turn can lead to hasty decisions—and render you ineffective.

Severance Benefits

Chances are you were instructed about all severance benefits due you during your exit interview with your old employer's personnel or human resources representative. If not, go through your company handbook or call your former employer to find out just what you have coming to you. For example, vacation time you didn't use, as well as any vested rights in profit-sharing or pension plans, is money due you. If you have the option of accepting payment in either a lump sum or in installments, check with your accountant before deciding which method is better for you.

The law says severed employees' final earnings checks must be paid promptly. In some states they must be given their last check by the next business day. Most stipulate that payment be made by the end of the current pay period. Call the nearest department of labor office for information on the situation in your state.

Health Insurance

You'll want to be sure your family is covered by medical and hospital insurance while you're between jobs. If your spouse is employed and covered, transfer to that active group policy. If you are single or your spouse is not employed, investigate the continuation of your existing group policy.

Public Law 99–272, enacted in 1986, requires that most employers sponsoring group health plans offer terminated employees and their families the opportunity to extend their health coverage at the prevailing group rate for an additional 18 months, if necessary. Employees who qualify have 60 days from the date they lose coverage to inform the plan administrator that they want continuation coverage.

Under this law (a mouthful called the Consolidated Omnibus Budget Reconciliation Act, or COBRA for short), employers enrolled in any of the nearly two million health plans affected must offer terminated employees coverage identical to what they previously had. Keep in mind that continuation coverage may cost you up to 102 percent of what it costs the employer, but still will be less expensive than getting coverage on your own.

If all of this comes as news to you, call your former company's personnel office for details. (If you can't get the information you need, contact the Pensions and Welfare Benefits Administration of the U.S. Department of Labor, which administers the law.)

If for some reason you are not covered by COBRA (your ex-employer has not paid the premium for continuation coverage, for example), you'll need to choose another alternative. You could ask for opinions from an insurance agent you trust, or spend a morning calling major carriers represented in your area.

Describe your situation and ask what they can do for you. Sign up for some high-deductible catastrophe term insurance at the very least, so you won't be wiped out if a family member is hospitalized for a major illness or accident. Get insurance to cover the essentials and be sure the policy is renewable in order to cover your maximum anticipated period of employment.

Unemployment Compensation

If you left your job involuntarily, you face a different set of problems—many of which were discussed in Chapter 1. On the plus side, you are probably eligible for unemployment benefits, financed jointly by your former employer and state and federal governments. If you feel the least bit uneasy about applying for unemployment benefits, keep in mind that your ex-employer contributed to the fund from which your checks will be drawn. Your work, in turn, contributed to your ex-employer's profits. So, you are indeed deserving of the money you receive.

If you have been employed long enough, and have earned sufficient wages (minimum standards will vary from state to state), you are eligible for unemployment benefits. In most states you can qualify for benefits unless you were fired for:

- Repeated willful conduct in disregard of your employer's interests, or

- A single act of willful misconduct that seriously endangers the life, safety, or property of your employer, a fellow employee, or the general public.[1]

The formula used to determine your maximum weekly benefit varies widely from state to state. First of all, your former employer pays 6.2 percent of the first $7,000 of every employee's income in federal unemployment taxes, or $434 a year. However, the employer gets a credit of up to 5.4 percent for *state* unemployment taxes already paid. If an employer pays 5.2 percent in state taxes, then, the bill to the feds will be only an additional 1 percent.

Similarly, maximum weekly payments vary by state. In Indiana the range is $140 to $181. In Massachusetts one can be paid anywhere from $312 to $468, depending on the previous full year's salary.[2]

You can see it is important to ask questions, no matter where you live. And, since the appropriate documents permitting you to file for unemployment insurance also vary from state to state, call your local unemployment office first to be sure you take the right

---

[1] A complete list of reasons for disqualifying a former employee from receiving unemployment compensation can be found in Appendix A.

[2] A table of "Current Minimum and Maximum Weekly Unemployment Benefit Amount By State," appears in Appendix B.

paperwork and identification with you on your first trip. Beyond this, to get your checks you must:

- File your claim for benefits.
- Sign up with your state job service.
- Be physically and mentally capable of working.
- Remain available for work and make a reasonable effort to get a job.

Payments are not retroactive to your first day of unemployment. They start with the date of your application. So don't get your search under way, then think you'll collect "back payments." If you need the cash, apply immediately. Although you will not be penalized for a late application in most states, you will only be paid for a predetermined amount of time or until you start your new job, whichever occurs first.

Unemployment insurance won't help you, however, if it expires before you apply. The deadline for this expiration is one other factor that varies from state to state, so be sure to apply as soon as you are eligible.

Cash Crunch

Conventional wisdom in dealing with a tight money situation is to duck your creditors for a while on the grounds that it will take them months to catch up with you, by which time you will be out of your mess.

The problem is, such a tactic only makes matters more ugly—exponentially. First come the stronger dunning letters; then the phone calls, some of them both insulting and embarrassing; then the personal visits; then the lawsuits and resulting panic.

There are ways to protect your credit history while sparing yourself and your family further upheaval. Contrary to what you've been told or have thought, most creditors will not only respect you for confronting your fiscal problems, but almost universally will be willing to work with you on a plan that permits you to stretch out your payments in manageable fashion. When creditors don't hear from you and your checks dry up, their logical conclusion is that you intend to stiff them. Not surprisingly, they go into action the only way they know how.

No matter what your financial condition, your first step should be to put together a cash flow chart to see exactly what monies are coming in and going out each month. Formulate action plans based on finding a job in three months, six months, nine months, and twelve months. (See Appendix C, for a model, and Appendix D, for a plan to cut expenses.)

Determine what bills you must pay in full, what bills you can pay partially, and what payments you can delay. Plan with your family what you can live without or with less of, so you can reduce your spending accordingly. If you own your own home, make an appointment with your banker to consider contingency plans—such as refinancing your mortgage, or reduced principal or interest-only mortgage payments—until you find a job.

For all other creditors—utilities, department stores, finance and credit card companies—write a letter describing your situation, propose a plan for payment, and do your best to stick with it. Doctors, dentists, and other independent professionals to whom you owe money probably will be willing to work out a minimum monthly payment arrangement.

Check your attic, garage, and basement for belongings to sell. What you find that others are willing to pay for will surprise you.

ORGANIZING YOUR OFFICE

Those of you between jobs who are also working with a full-service outplacement facility can skip to the "Setting up your files" section on page 33. The rest of you should be interested in what follows.

The first step is to choose a space that can serve as headquarters for the duration of your job search. Working out of your home will be much less expensive than renting an office, but may involve other logistical difficulties. Only you can tell.

In either case, it is difficult to run an office from an attaché case or the kitchen table. What is required is a room from which you can conduct your business without interruption.

An exception, offered here not just to prove the rule but to show necessity mothering a little innovation, involves a Manhattan magazine executive acquaintance who managed his job search from a small Greek restaurant owned by a friend. Weekdays one summer from 10:00 to 11:00 A.M. and 3:00 to 5:00 P.M., his office was a back table near the phone. During the busy lunch hours his friend the owner answered the phone without blowing his cover. By the time

Labor Day came around, fortunately, the job seeker had two offers.

Most of us, even with friends as helpful and minds as fertile as this, are probably better off with more domestically centered solutions. For example: Do you have a daughter away at college? Usable or convertible space in the cellar or attic? Younger children who can double up to free a bedroom for a few months? A common room, such as a parlor or dining room, that you can commandeer for the job-search duration?

Selecting a Desk

Discussing one's desk choice in a job-search book may seem trivial, but it is not. Some of the most important decisions of your professional life could be made in your home office. It is essential that your organizational priorities include any details that facilitate your ability to make these decisions.

To cover the most obvious first, you need a large working surface and sufficient file drawers to have available those materials you need at a second's notice, as well as storage space for materials you are not working with on a given day.

If you don't have a suitable desk, check used furniture stores nearby. The business losses and downsizings that have cost so many Americans their jobs have also produced a glut of serviceable furniture, computers, and other office equipment. If your resources are severely limited, a large piece of 3/4-inch plywood can serve, set on top of as many plastic milk cases as will give you the right height and enough file space.

Desk design is important. You may want two or three working surfaces: one for writing, with room for reference materials and notes; one for your telephone and answering machine, with room for phone notes; and one for your word processor or personal computer. This degree of flexibility will allow you to switch gears without excessive downtime for setting up and taking down.

This is your private office and should be organized for maximum efficiency as long as you need it. You also should be comfortable here, primarily to keep your energy level high. Decorate for eye appeal only to the extent that it contributes to your morale. If you have small children, work out a set of rules that allows you privacy during the time you need it most, but with scheduled breaks so as not to shut out the rest of the family. You need their support during this time as much as they need yours.

Phone Service

For the best communications base, consider a telephone service that stretches your capability. Mountain Bell and Pacific Bell call it "Custom Calling"; Southern New England Telephone calls it "Totalphone." Whatever the label in your calling area, this service costs little and allows you to:

- Deal with two or more calls simultaneously without losing "caller number one"

- Initiate or participate in a conference call

- Forward calls to a second number when you're away from the phone or not at home.

Custom calling is available in many areas for less than $10 a month plus a one-time installation charge—but varies, depending on your location. In some areas, for example, the conference call option is not available or costs extra. In others, the company will throw in a "speed calling" option, for example, through which you can preprogram 10 or more phone numbers and be connected by dialing a single digit plus "#."

For an additional $75 to $100 you may want to consider installing an answering machine to retrieve your messages while you are away. More impressive—and usually more expensive, depending on where you live—is a personal answering service providing a live voice to take messages, let callers know where you are, how long you'll be away, and how to get in touch with you. Figure an additional $45 to $100 for such a service. Many who provide it will also type your letters and provide mailing assistance, charging either by the hour or by the piece.

Those of you in a recent termination situation lucky enough to have been assigned an outplacement company will have neither a telephone nor an office problem. You should, however, find out how the phone is being answered. Some larger outplacement facilities offer a sophisticated enough phone system to afford individualized answering at the switchboard: "Good morning. Jack Fuller's office." Often, however, this level of personalization is available only to higher level executives. For most, the answer is likely to be some variation of: "Executive offices. How may I direct your call?"

Most callers hearing such a response will catch on immediately that they're talking to an outplacement firm, or at least that they are being mildly deceived in some way. This is not itself the kiss of death, to be sure, because these days outplacement is an experience shared by many. The point is that many individuals recently out of work have not yet come to terms with their unemployment—some to the extent that they even deny being unemployed. Our advice, in light of the fact that responses such as the above from "your" outplacement company are likely to fool no one, is to be honest enough to avoid any such pretense. Your cover is blown, in all likelihood, and any attempt to pretend you are employed when you are not will certainly backfire on you.

Transitional Phone Instructions

Until your home or outplacement office is set up properly, you need to be sure your messages reach you in a timely fashion. Call your former office every few days to see how requests to speak with you are being handled. Make sure your switchboard operator (including all relief operators), as well as anyone likely to answer your old extension, says: "He can be reached at [your new office number]," *without elaboration or explanation.* To be sure this happens, ask friendly former co-workers to follow through on your behalf. A terse "he doesn't work here anymore," followed by a click, will not advance your job search measurably.

Here is one other phone-related tip: Invest in a spindle or book-type phone directory in which you keep—near your phone—all job-search-related phone numbers and addresses. Get in the habit of keeping pencil and paper at the ready to record incoming messages and to avoid having to say: "Can you hang on for a minute? I have to find a pen," which will label you as less organized than the average job seeker.

Setting Up Your Files

When you are looking for a job full time, you need two sets of files. One should be organized by job prospect, the other arranged by time. However, if you are looking for a job on a part-time basis and already have a system for keeping all your follow-up and administrative files in order, you'll need only prospect files to keep you organized.

If you have set up and maintained files at some other point in your career, you may wish to skip this section. If you have not, some of the following techniques represent the kind of secretarial secrets that have contributed to the "back-office" success of many executives.

Prospect Files

All the papers regarding individual prospects should be kept together. When you review this information, all of the research, annual report and company literature, notes from reconnaissance interviews, telephone interview notes, correspondence, and the like should be where you can compare, evaluate, or prepare as necessary. This level of organization will help you avoid the dangerous practice of depending solely on your memory to make important job-search decisions. When a file grows too thick to be easily handled, divide it into two "Current" and "Background" folders.

As to a few obvious, but frequently overlooked considerations:

- Don't use your file folder as a note pad. If you need to write something down, use a piece of paper and add the note to your folder.

- When you receive a business card of possible future use, copy it, add the information to the appropriate prospect file(s), and put the original in your spindle directory (or whatever trademarked version you own). Don't staple the card to your folder.

- Your file folder should look new and professional. When you leave your office for an interview, you should be able to slip the right folder into your carrying case. This way you will be able to review all related material while you wait and to pull out a pertinent document during the interview for reference if need be.

If this last point is new to you, remember that you need to exhibit many of the same kinds of professionalism in your interviews that you would on the job—if the interviewer were your boss. For example, you should feel comfortable referencing, say, a magazine article relevant to your conversation, every bit as readily in an interview as you would in a staff meeting; even offer your interviewer the opportunity to copy the article if she wishes. More about avoiding the interviewee's traditionally defeatist attitude

("I'm not okay; I'm a candidate") in the companion book *Conquer Interview Objections.*

Tickler Files

This is the perfect organizer for the job hunter who spends a few hours at his desk several days a week, supplementing as it does a pocket calendar that lists all scheduled commitments. The tickler file cross-references the pocket calendar, reminding you of all the administrative preparation and follow-up you must complete to assure the success of all your scheduled meetings.

If you haven't seen a tickler file, visualize:

1. Thirty-one files labeled in numerical order from "1" to "31," for each day of the month;
2. Twelve files labeled for the months of the year, set up chronologically behind the daily files;
3. Two files for the next two years, set up behind the monthly files.

Here's how the tickler system works: Today is May 10, 1995. Bruce Bergquist has agreed to meet you for a cup of coffee "in a month or so" to discuss prospects at a company he knows about and you're interested in. Write yourself a note to call Bruce the first week of June to confirm the appointment and add any other key details, including questions you've thought to ask. Place these notes in the June folder, just behind the "31" in the daily folder.

At the end of May, take out the June folder. Refile all of your June notes in the daily folders, as indicated. Put the empty June folder behind all of the other monthly folders, just behind May and in front of the two yearly files.

You look at your notes for your meeting with Bruce, and put them in the "3" slot (June 3 is Monday of the first week in the month), as a reminder to make your confirmation call on that day.

Every day you come to the office you can open the file for that day and see at a glance what job-search-related activities you have scheduled for that day. A good technique to practice is to go through the folder for any given day just before you leave the office the day before, as a base for compiling your To Do list for that day.

Learn to rely completely on your Tickler File. If you have a meeting that requires overnight travel, put the flight tickets in the jacket for the day you are to leave. If you have to do research prior to an interview, put a note in the file far enough ahead of time to give you sufficient time to prepare.

Write down everything you want to remember, and file it by date. This should include not only what you must do, but any good ideas you might come up with about how to do them. For example, if you know that you are meeting Bruce Bergquist to learn more about careers in the health care industry, your brain will begin to work on this opportunity immediately—even though you may be focusing on other things. If you have a sudden great idea or question about health care, you can write it down and file it in the appropriate slot, even though you are working on a completely different matter.

If you are going to be on the road for five days, take the files for those days with you, along with the folder for your first day back in the office. Most business travelers find themselves with an hour or more to kill in an airport or in the hotel room between meetings, which provides plenty of time for returning phone calls or initiating those that have been promised.

Pocket Calendar

For those few of you who do not already have a calendar to carry with you, invest a few dollars to get one. They're available in most stationery stores, many small enough to fit in a shirt pocket.

ORGANIZING YOUR DAY

You have at least two sources for organizing any particular day: the tickler file and your pocket calendar. Your task is to organize every day into a challenging, but achievable, list of things to do. This section offers an approach for doing just that.

Either last thing at night or first thing in the morning, take a fresh piece of paper and put the hours of your workday down the left-hand margin, with plenty of space in between. View this list as a guide, however, rather than as production specifications.

Previous Commitments

Write up all job-search-related appointments already scheduled—for example, reconnaissance, networking, and job interviews. When you discover a conflict, your first priority is the job interview. Call everybody else and reschedule.

When scheduling, allow for transportation time, including a safety margin for unforeseen difficulties. If you've scheduled more than one interview in a morning or afternoon, take into consideration the fact that meetings sometimes start late or run over, or that you might be asked to speak with one or more people in addition to your principal interviewer.

"It actually happened" department: The manager of college recruiting for a *Fortune* 500 company received a call in the middle of her hiring interview from another candidate waiting in the lobby. He needed to see her immediately, or risk being late for an interview across town with another company. She excused herself, interrupting the ongoing interview, and went to the lobby to spend several minutes with the other candidate, ultimately encouraging him to go to his next interview. The unsurprising upshot is that he was not invited back.

The moral is: Build time cushions into your interview schedules; everything takes longer than you think it will.

Telephone Calls

After scheduling your search-related appointments and any other personal commitments that are unavoidable, set aside a block of time for telephone calls. Don't try to make it easy on yourself by spreading your calls out over the business day, two or three an hour. It is impossible to be effective this way and leaves too little time at the end of the day for calls to be returned.

Let's face it; these calls are hard work. It's always tough to communicate without being able to read facial expressions or body language. It's even tougher when you're calling strangers (the dreaded "cold call"); and toughest of all when you have to get past an intermediary to reach your calling target. (See Chapter 4 for telephone marketing tips.)

For many, making phone calls is the most onerous part of the job search. If this is you, schedule your difficult calls before you do anything else—or you'll never make them at all.

Do whatever it takes to psyche yourself into a calling mood. Some people make a low-risk call first to get them on a roll. Others make the toughest call first. (Do you ease yourself into the water before a morning swim, or dive straight into the lake?)

Telephone Tactics

- The best way to schedule your telephone period is all at once. Normally, you should start about 8:15 A.M. to catch people at their desk planning *their* days, before the meetings begin and before secretaries arrive to screen calls.

- Most outgoing calls should be completed by 9:30. This way, you can be working while you wait for your call-backs and put your time to the best use.

- If you have early morning appointments, initiate your calls for the day after you return. Don't ask people to return your calls if you're not going to be there to take them. Even if you have someone taking your messages, people hate to return a call they "just missed," only to discover that their caller was not considerate enough to wait a few minutes until they returned the call as asked.

- Other good times to catch busy people are 12:30–1:00 P.M., for those who eat lunch at their desks, and after 5:30 P.M., when meetings are over and presumably the next day's planning has begun.

- Always be clear in your mind about the purpose of your call and how you are going to achieve it. Preparation is the key element in your success—including keeping all of your data (correspondence, notes, and materials for taking notes) in front of you for ready reference. (For more on telephone marketing, see Chapter 4. For more on "Overcoming Objections," see Chapter 4, in *Conquer Interview Objections*.)

- Don't always leave a message—or even your name. In some instances it is easier to manage a conversation to your advantage if the recipient is not ready for your call. If your target knows you are going to call and what you want, this information gives her more time to prepare objections.

- If your party is not in, ask for her probable return time and call back then. (Assuming you don't reach an electronic mailbox—on which you *never* leave a message—you can ask for a better time to call again.)

- Don't leave long messages with a secretary or receptionist who doesn't know you. These people are usually extremely busy and sometimes handle hundreds of calls a day.

- If you have built a relationship with a well-positioned secretary or assistant by being more pleasant or polite than the average caller, you have increased your chances of getting a message through to your target.

- Remember that you are trying with every phone call to develop a professional relationship with the callee. Even though you are a great face-to-face interviewer, your telephone tactics could prevent your ever getting to that stage.

Your Daily Schedule

Now you can schedule the rest of your To Do list with whatever research, correspondence, or follow-up is dictated by your tickler file for the day.

Some of the items in your file may no longer be relevant. If so, throw them away. But be careful about any item you repeatedly put off until another day. Confront it. Either throw it away or deal with it that day.

Schedule the tasks you consider less pleasant first, so you won't have to face them later in the day, when you may be less fresh.

Following is a model daily schedule representing a typical day in the life of an active job seeker. Use it as a way of prioritizing your activities, keeping in mind that no two days will be alike, but that all of them need to be scheduled.

Morning

7:00–8:15   Breakfast meeting: Reconnaissance interview to consolidate observations about a target company. If no meeting, complete all preparations for morning phone calls.

8:15–9:30   Make cold calls to companies, based on library research the previous day. Telephone all targeted company executives with whom you have established initial contact, and all others otherwise requiring telephone contact.

9:30–11:30   Initiate all correspondence to target companies identified through research; take return phone calls as dictated; schedule any indicated interviews.

11:30–12:00   Prepare agenda for luncheon meeting.

12:30–2:00	If no luncheon meeting has been scheduled, use this time for spot phone calls, library research on target companies, or an exercise break.
2:00–2:30	Return missed phone calls; complete noon hour research.
2:30–4:30	Finish and proofread letters written that morning.
4:30–5:30	Make and return all remaining phone calls; with the aid of your tickler file and research, prepare notes for the next day's phone calls.
5:30–6:00	Stop. If you have adhered to your schedule, you have put in an honest day's effort. If you had no bites it was because the fish weren't biting, not that you didn't use the right tackle.

CELEBRATING YOUR VICTORIES

Getting organized also has to do with such an elemental consideration as what might be called "keeping your head on straight." Confidence and morale are two crucial commodities job seekers sometimes have in diminished supply. It's easy to blame oneself—often unjustly—when interviews and job offers dry up. The inevitable consequence is a loss of both confidence *and* morale, usually followed by a sharp drop in job-search effectiveness.

A job search is stressful, especially if cash flow is a problem. But if you think you must work until midnight five or more days a week to get a job, it will never happen. The tenseness that finally overcomes you will lead you into stupid and embarrassing mistakes, and will adversely affect relationships with those around you.

One problem is that progress is difficult to measure in a job search. Sometimes a promising situation resulting in a number of progressively successful interviews will be broken off for no discernible reason. This can be a frustrating, devastating, and—in some instances—a long-lasting experience.

In any case, a course correction is in order. Work out a system that will allow you to appreciate the smaller, day-to-day accomplishments easily overlooked if your thoughts are consumed by your ultimate goal. If you set and reach a production goal every day, you can leave the office knowing you did a good day's work.

Stretch yourself. Make the job tough, but attainable. Take pride in accomplishing these quotas, even though your tangible rewards are not yet in sight.

Monday's goal could be:

- Two introductory letters to target companies
- Follow-up on all outstanding phone calls
- One face-to-face business meeting (reconnaissance or networking interview; see *Conquer Interview Objections*)
- Research three target companies.

If you are searching for a new job and are still employed, your goal could be to add one new target company per week, including all necessary phone follow-up, correspondence, and research. Resist the temptation to work late every night to give your "second job" equal weight. You need the restorative energy that comes with proper rest and relaxation.

Speaking of which, if you are physically fit—for example, weigh what you want to weigh—chances are you will be mentally fit as well, and be able to convey the positive feeling so much a part of those who are in command of themselves. (Surveys indicate that one of the greatest negative discrimination factors in job interviews is obesity. If you are overweight, this is a perfect time to do something about it—but first see a qualified counselor.) In job search you probably have more control over your daily schedule than at any other time in your professional career and thus should be able to work out a physical fitness and diet program that will keep you in top physical and mental shape.

Remember that your spouse, children, friends, and relatives are under stress, too. Likely they'll mirror your moods. If you're upbeat and relaxed after a day of job hunting, they'll be relaxed, too. When you're late and uptight, it will be reflected in them—and escalate if nervousness becomes the norm.

Bring your family in on the problem to promote a team effort and to keep resentment, fear, and frustration down. Share both your successes and your disappointments (without overemphasizing the latter). Paying closer attention to your family will neutralize one of the more difficult aspects of job search: loneliness.

The general principal is to set "stretch goals" that are attainable, and reward yourself as you accomplish them. For example, after every job interview, have dinner out—even at an inexpensive neighborhood restaurant, if that's all you can afford. Take an occasional afternoon off to watch your daughter or nephew play ball. If you've worked hard the rest of the week, you've earned a break.

A Danish house painter tells how he celebrates small victories. While painting a new Copenhagen hotel, for example, he put one bottle of cold beer at the end of the long corridors for each painter in the crew. When they finished painting a corridor, they took their well-deserved break.

Put treats at the end of your corridors—and stay motivated.

ADDITIONAL READING

Hedrick, Lucy. *Five Days to an Organized Life.* New York: Dell Trade Paperback, 1990. Clear goals; bite-sized objectives; time management; celebrating successes.

Scott, Robert. *Office at Home.* New York: Scribner's, 1985. Advice on everything from budgeting and bookkeeping to decorating and suppliers; separation of home and business activities.

3

The Flexible Resume

The resume is considered by many a necessary evil, a wordy calling card offered to recruiters and prospective employers with the hope that it will impress and lead to the interview that spawns the job offer. Some career counselors look upon resumes with scorn, and advise their clients to use them only on demand. Yet with few exceptions, everyone who wants a job has to have a resume.

Why this ambivalence? Much of it has to do with the uneven quality of the millions of resumes in circulation. Writing a resume is an onerous task, disposed of quickly by most job seekers to get more quickly to the "real" part of job search. Because these finished products reflect the level of effort that went into them, it can only mean that a lot of people every year get jobs in spite of their resumes, rather than because of them. Others hype the deeds of their writers with a level of hyperbole that justifies the suspicion with which they are read. (A few "before" and "after" examples representing both these categories appear in Chapter 5.)

The present job situation in this country, described earlier in this book and elsewhere as well, complicates matters considerably. It isn't enough any more for job seekers to have a single all-purpose resume out there spreading the word for them. One of the small edges a candidate can create is to individualize his marketing effort to every target company, including the preparation of a tailored resume presenting a profile that mirrors—insofar as possible—each open position.

Enter the "flexible resume," which brings us to the following three points and the focus of the rest of the chapter:

1. Take as much time as necessary to create the best possible "master resume;"

2. Maintain a *flexible* resume you can adjust as necessary for maximum impact in your job marketing;

3. Create a master cover letter that you can adapt for specific job opportunities.

THE MASTER RESUME

The much maligned resume actually is a multipurpose tool, crucial to your job search. Here are some of the ways a resume can act in your behalf:

- As an advance communicator that helps employers match your strengths to their needs and decide whether there is reason enough to offer an invitation to interview.

- As a professional brochure, distributed to prospective professional colleagues for reference and evaluation of your professional skills, accomplishments, promotions, and career highlights.

- As a reflection of your "sense of self" through its content, form, and style.

There is another important role a resume plays—less tangible than those mentioned above, but no less significant. The process of researching, writing, and refining one's professional life in the strongest and most comprehensive way can be both a liberating and an enlightening experience. It can also be a confidence builder at a time when your confidence could use a boost.

Most people underestimate the sheer volume of accomplishments and responsibilities they have amassed in a professional lifetime. Organizing so many career-related details to maximum advantage can be a great spirit-lifter. It also can contribute significantly to a successful interview. If you have researched your background well, you'll be able to describe even long-ago accomplishments in ways that coincide, say, with an interviewer's prospective assignment. Relying on your memory alone in such a situation, however, is likely to lead to a much more random, inaccurate, and counter-productive response.

The Pros Rate Resumes

Not long ago we conducted a survey of more than 50 metropolitan New York area corporate line managers, human resource professionals, and recruiters who had read enough resumes that, laid end to end, they would reach from Xerox corporate headquarters in southern Connecticut to its Transamerica equivalent in San Francisco. (Just a guess, mind you.)

What we wanted to know was, what resume characteristics did these pros consider "good," and what "bad." Here are a few of the questions we asked:

- How many resumes do you receive a day?
- How much time do you take to read each one?
- What determines how much time you spend on each one?
- How long do you believe a resume should be?
- What information do you think a resume should convey?
- What resume format do you prefer (chronological, functional, other)?
- How would you define a "good" resume?
- How would you define a "bad" resume?
- What do you think are the most frequent mistakes people make when writing resumes?

Although answers varied widely to a number of these questions, the point about which there was virtual unanimity among the survey respondents was that whatever other qualities a resume did or did not have, it must communicate—totally and instantly. In those instances where a large number of applicants are in line for a position, for example, the experts agree that 10 or 15 seconds may be as long as each resume has to communicate the most significant job-related strengths.

In such a situation one can't count on a principal interviewer to read between the lines. Because of the size of the potential talent pool (for some widely advertised jobs, several hundred responses are not unusual), a number of first readers probably have been assigned to screen the resumes against a checklist jointly prepared by the hiring manager and the human resources department. (Understandably, to get to the bottom of their resume stacks, readers find themselves looking to *ex*clude rather than *in*clude applicants—and the sooner the better.)

If the vice president of manufacturing wants to hire a director of purchasing, for example, she may specify five essential qualities first readers should look for. During the first week of screening, she may require that at least four of these five qualities be identifiable in the resume. Those attributes difficult to pick up, or perhaps expressed in wording unfamiliar to the reader, are judged to be nonexistent—and out goes the resume.

Resume Formats

There are several resume formats commonly used by job seekers. Only two, however, Chronological and Functional (with a couple of variations of each), exist in enough profusion to discuss in any detail.

The basic difference between them is that the chronological resume ties one's accomplishments and responsibilities closely to specific positions and employers, and the functional resume organizes this same information by skill groupings, irrespective of job or employer. Frequently a list of positions held, with inclusive dates, appears on the second page of the resume, with no elaboration or attempt to correlate it with the data that preceded it. Some functional resumes include no dates whatsoever.

The chronological format (actual *reverse* chronological because jobs are listed present-day first) is the easiest to follow (except when badly done), and gives a much better picture of the candidate's direction, professional history, and promotion record. The functional resume is often used to paper over a professional blemish or gap in one's record. For example:

- A spotty work record, with frequent changes of employers
- A substantive career change, in which certain of one's skills or accomplishments—but not the function or industry in which they were attained—would be of interest to the prospective employer
- A re-entry into a career area after time away freelancing, consulting, raising children, or unemployed.

The problem with a functional resume is that although it does its job of repackaging for any reason applicable to the situation, it also stigmatizes by implying to the wary reader (more and more of them these days), that something is not quite right. And if your cover letter hasn't illuminated the situation with sufficient candor, your candidacy is dead.

The downside of a chronological resume? A job hopper or a 63-year-old applicant, among others, risks immediate rejection as his perceived warts begin to emerge (in reverse chronological order). The way out is to always tell the truth, but to avoid revealing information about yourself that is potentially damaging. In some instances a hybrid combining the best of both styles will be best for you.

Organizing Your Resume

All of this accountability is a heavy burden for a resume, which means that it must be written with extreme care. Writing of any kind is difficult. As William Zinsser says in *On Writing Well,* "A clear sentence is no accident. Very few sentences come out right the first time. . . . [Writing] is one of the hardest things people do."

Writing resumes can be harder than just about any other kind of writing. One reason is that *you have to put your entire professional life on one or two pages. Not only that, you have to make it interesting and attractive.* Talk about pressure.

Actually, writing is only part of the job of making a really good resume. It almost needs to be constructed or crafted, as well as written. All its pieces must interlock in seamless fashion, with meticulous attention paid to what has gone before and what comes next.

The various elements of a candidate that an employer may be looking for (upward mobility, tangible accomplishments, stability, and the like) must pop out and catch the reader's eye. Some of this can be accomplished, as you will see, by the creative use of type and white space.

By underlining, using boldface or italics, or putting key words or phrases in capital letters—all done in a consistent, systematic way—different elements of a resume can be made more visible. Similarly, by putting some "air" between entries, or by spacing some kinds of data vertically or horizontally from others, all of the elements can be made easier to read, and more data can be taken in easily at a single reading. For example, two- to four-line entries are far easier to read than dense paragraphs of type, and are therefore far more likely to *get* read. (For "before" and "after" examples, see Chapter 5.)

To reach this level of quality, be prepared to write several drafts, working much like a chef reducing a multi-ingredient liquid to a delicate sauce. "Omit needless words," was William Strunk's advice in *The Elements of Style*. Although Strunk's focus was writing in general, it could easily have been narrowed to just resume writing.

Resume Nitty-gritty

Participants in the resume survey mentioned earlier were specific about those resume elements they thought were essential. For convenience we have grouped their responses into three categories: Content, Clarity, and Appearance. Following are those about which there was general agreement:

Content

- Position yourself in a way that enables the reader to identify both your short- and long-term goals.
- Stress your accomplishments for each job in quantitative terms where possible, as well as in terms of the specific nature of the job.
- Organize your resume in such a way that your professional level is clearly evident. If you have more than three years of job experience, for example, the "Education" section should come at the end of your resume.
- Load the resume in favor of accomplishments, skills, and responsibilities that relate specifically to the job you are seeking. Quantify where possible.
- Eliminate all but essential personal data.
- Avoid detailed descriptions of previous jobs; the further back in time, the less detail.
- Be truthful about problem areas such as employment gaps and perceived job-hopping, but avoid including gratuitous, potentially damaging information.
- Include all career-related volunteer experience.

Clarity

- For ease of reading, limit all descriptions of jobs and accomplishments to four lines or less.
- State your position objective and experience summary clearly and specifically.
- Double check to eliminate errors or inconsistencies in grammar or punctuation. If necessary, ask an English teacher, librarian, or local newspaper editor for help.
- Clearly identify all personal data (name, address, and phone numbers).
- State your job history in reverse chronological order, making sure that multiple positions for the same company are not mistaken for separate employers.

Appearance

- Invest in quality typing (or typesetting) and printing job.
- Choose paper of good weight and quality (Strathmore or Classic Laid); standard size (8 1/2" x 11"); and conservative color (white, ivory, or gray).
- Avoid attention-motivated special effects (mixed type faces, brochure format, photographs, or cartoons).
- Limit your resume length to two pages.
- Keep the "look" of your resume appropriate to the position level you are seeking (a typeset resume for an entry-level candidate will look ostentatious).
- Take all measures necessary to eliminate typographical errors. If necessary, pay an expert to proofread for you.
- Be consistent throughout the resume regarding any stylistic decisions you make (the use or non-use of periods after each entry, for example).

Write to a Target Audience

Good writers write for specific audiences. As a resume writer, your audience will depend on how widely you are casting your net. The wider the cast, the more variations you'll need. And if you intend to "cross over" to another industry or function, you'll need to think about additional resumes that may bear little resemblance to your original resume.

Your goal is to address your reader's specific needs. To do this you must be able to communicate three fundamental levels of information:

1. Knowledge of industry
2. Knowledge of company
3. Knowledge of position or function

Knowledge of industry. If you are re-entering the marketplace at the level you left it—or above—you must demonstrate your awareness of industry trends, problems, and promise, including any state-of-the-art responsibilities you have held or accomplishments you have attained. An example of a resume with this kind of emphasis appears in Chapter 5.

Knowledge of company. This level of awareness usually can be demonstrated in terms of the company you just left or for which you are now employed. After all, if you are changing very little about your career, a number of similarities will exist between your last company and your next one. Your knowledge of other companies can be handled in the cover letters that accompany the resumes you send these companies. See examples later in this chapter and in the second book, *Conquer Interview Objections*.

Knowledge of position or function. If you are moving up a notch, the job you want will probably be very much like the one your boss or ex-boss has. In this case, you need to be sure your *prospective* boss can see which of your *past* boss's responsibilities you either have handled or can handle. This is the simplest way of going about the task, obviously. Those of you changing functions, industries, or both, will find it tougher. Still, the strategy remains the same.

RESUME COMPONENTS

The most effective resume will consist of an Objective; a Summary or Profile; a listing of all pertinent professional Experience; Education; and career-related hobbies; licenses, certifications, and affiliations.

The Objective

The first two sections of your resume, the Objective and the Summary, will set the tone for all of the information that follows. These two entries, when carefully written, can influence the reader to the extent that they affect the way everything else in the resume is perceived.

Above the Objective, of course, you must identify yourself by name, address, and phone number(s). This information should be prominent and clearly positioned. Keep your name the same as the one on your driver's license. That your friends or family call you "Skip" or "Lefty" will be of minimal interest to a prospective employer.

Write an Objective that reflects the job for which you are applying as closely as possible. A simple, concise title is best, because you immediately position yourself for the open slot. Here are a few examples:

OBJECTIVE:	Director of Purchasing
OBJECTIVE:	Senior Mathematics Editor
OBJECTIVE:	Marketing/Sales Manager
OBJECTIVE:	Financial Analyst
OBJECTIVE:	Public Affairs Officer

Don't waste time, postage, or paper on mushy, unfocused appeals such as these real-life, not-made-up examples from our files:

OBJECTIVE: A responsible and challenging position that will allow me to utilize my education, experience, and personal abilities to achieve business success.

(Or: Companies offering irresponsible, nonchallenging positions need not respond.)

OBJECTIVE: To leverage developed skills and accumulated knowledge in a challenging senior management role, with the scope, authority, and resources to make major impact.

(Or: I want no replies from companies whose practice it is to utilize undeveloped skills and nonaccumulated knowledge.)

OBJECTIVE: To obtain a position in an environment that allows and encourages professional growth and unlimited income potential.

(Or: All you environments without deep pockets and that discourage professional growth, forget about it.)

The bad advice these candidates received regarding Objective writing cost them interview opportunities and, ultimately, job offers, because they were perceived to be completely lacking focus— or at least unable to express their Objectives in an effective manner.

In situations where you have not been able to precisely pinpoint the job title, broaden your base slightly to appeal to a narrow band of positions, but not so broadly that you risk making the same error as the three resume writers so shamelessly ridiculed above. Be as specific as you can be by *function*, because the same job often goes by a number of different titles in company within an industry.

If, at any given target company, there is the possibility of a job opportunity *in addition to the one for which you are applying*, it may be advisable to omit the Objective and go right on to your Summary. Specificity in this case could be a liability rather than an asset. Similarly, when supplying a resume to an executive recruiter or employment agency, eliminate your Objective so as not to box yourself in.

The Summary

The purpose of the Objective is to mirror as closely as possible the open position. The Summary (or "Profile," or "Professional Highlights") tells why you are qualified to fill it. Your goal is to put together as strong a statement as you can combining *position-related* accomplishments, skills, and special qualifications for the job. Keep the entry to three or four sentences that distill your professional experience into a single, compelling power statement. (In Chapter 4 we'll show you how to look at the Summary with a marketing emphasis and tie it to the "benefits" an employer looks for in considering your candidacy.)

The Summary is your opportunity to harness "the best of the best"—those aspects of your career (always in light of the Objective above it, which in turn reflects the specific job you are seeking) that will generate enough interest for the reader to schedule an interview. A job-related accomplishment you are proud of, but which occurred seven years and two jobs ago, can be positioned here where it will do you the most good. Placed in traditional context it would have appeared in the middle of page two and never been read, especially by a first reader giving it a quick once-over.

To write your summary, review your career to date and list all of the responsibilities, accomplishments, and skills you think will qualify you for this next position.

Following is a form that will help you construct your Summary:

What abilities or skills are needed for someone to be successful in the position listed in your Objective?

1. _____

2. _____

3. _____

4. _____

5. _____

In terms of the position you are seeking, what significant accomplishments highlighted your last three (if relevant, four) positions?

Most Recent Position

Title _____

Overall Duties

1. _____

2. _____

3. _____

4. _____

5. _____

Significant Achievement

Problem_____

_____

Action Taken _____

_____

_____

_____

Results (Quantify, if possible) _____

_____

_____

_____

_____

Key Skills Demonstrated

_____

_____

_____

_____

List as many problems as you can think of for which you significantly contributed action that led to tangible results. Specifically mention, for example, any situations or conditions you helped to improve, money you helped the company earn or save, any ideas you contributed that were adopted by the company, or any ways in which you increased sales. Repeat this process for each additional job that will yield potential job-related accomplishments or skills.

Now go back over everything you've done, circling those duties, accomplishments, and skills that relate most closely to the job listed in your Objective. Eliminate or combine all duplications or overlaps and group your qualifications by category. Rewrite this combined list, killing all unnecessary words and phrases. Utilize an "outline" style, omitting all articles and personal pronouns, as in the examples on pages 68–91.

Using the remaining circled items, write a first draft of your Summary. Share your draft with someone who knows your professional background. Use the resulting feedback to write a second draft of your Summary.

Look at what you've written. Is it interesting? Is it clear? Is it the right length? Are the ideas linked logically? Write as many drafts as it takes for you to be satisfied with the results.

Those of you considering a slight career change should keep in mind that the language you use in your resume is as important as the ideas conveyed. Change all applicable terminology from your old career to that of your new one. If you are a career military officer or noncom, for example, find a savvy civilian to eliminate all military acronyms and otherwise demilitarize what you've written.

Prospective employers don't see the crossover value of experience expressed in unfamiliar terms, even if it's right on target. They're trained to react and respond positively to their own industry's buzz words, and negatively to those outside the Club— sad but true.

An analogous point to remember for those of you changing careers: Avoid any mention of your former industry or function when cataloguing the great works comprising your Summary. Stay with "pure" strengths to avoid tainting your resume in this key section. Then, when it comes time to list your experience, there will be less stigma involved regarding where you did what you did. For example:

> SUMMARY: Fourteen years experience in sales and service of major industrial and commercial accounts. Ranked first in 12-person force three consecutive years. Outstanding record acquiring direct accounts and initiating client contact at top management levels. Comprehensive background conceptualizing and executing print and media advertising campaigns.

Such a record would cause more then one prospective employer to take a chance on this candidate, even if he were trying to get out of the nuclear waste removal industry.

Errol Sull, president of a career counseling firm that specializes in helping former prison inmates find jobs after their time is served, tells clients (many of whom are often making some of the most extreme career changes) to similarly stress generic strengths. Here is a version he suggests for a skilled embezzler trying to make it on the outside:

> SUMMARY: Excellent accounting skills; patient; well-organized; detail-oriented; professional demeanor; hands-on computer experience; goal-setter; resourceful; work well with little supervision.

Experience

In a chronological resume, the beef is the organization and presentation of specific jobs you've held in various companies. If you haven't heard this before, *a simple job description will not suffice.*

What a prospective employer wants to know is not only what you did, but how well you performed in each position. This means accomplishments, keyed to specific jobs and responsibilities. For these, go back to the Problem/Action/Results format you used to write your Summary.

Caveat: Don't write up accomplishments as your own that were in fact shared with other members of a team. Under close questioning, any hyperbole will come back to bite you, and probably knock you out of the running if in fact you had minimal responsibility for an achievement you are claiming as yours alone.

Treat past achievements consistent with your present career direction, and spend as few words as possible on aspects of previous positions that have no bearing on the kind of job you want today. Similarly, devote more attention to current or recent career-related positions than to those held earlier in your professional life. Don't appear to be dwelling on the past. Given two similar accomplishments reached both early in your career and recently, devote more attention to the second instance (closer to the *top* of the resume, after all) than the first.

Exception: If you are trying to get back into a career you followed when you were younger, put all of your early positions, accomplishments, and responsibilities under a heading such as "RELEVANT EXPERIENCE," and space them to fill the first page of your resume. This way your entire page one presentation will consist of an Objective, a Summary, and *only* that experience of appeal to a prospective employer.

Your problem is that employment dates for the job experience you're describing may go back a decade or more. Defuse this with a prominently placed monition, such as: "For Current Experience, see page 2"; or, "Most recent experience appears on following page."

Break up your Experience entries into sight-bites an interviewer can absorb quickly. Consider your resume as a *script*, for both you and the interviewer. Each entry, then, will be a *cue* for rehearsing a 10-second to 10-minute response, depending on your interviewer's interest.

For this reason, list your most impressive accomplishments in order of importance—almost the way you wrote a topic outline in your first high school composition course. Where possible, quantify your accomplishments to make them stronger. Follow a main point with appropriate subpoints, as did the textbook marketing executive profiled below:

- Directed marketing staff of 49, including product management, advertising and promotion, marketing and customer services.
- Implemented direct marketing techniques and aggressive pricing strategy to produce six times normal markup and over $2 million in annual sales of niche product line.
- Established telemarketing program with annual sales of $3.4 million; maintained reorders of $2.6 million consumable product line through annual phone campaign.
- Formulated successful marketing plan for launch of new flagship product line; restored lost market leadership with 18 percent market share gain.

Through careful writing and creative layout, make all key aspects of every entry as clear and as visible as possible. Your reader should be able to take in your strengths at a single glance and select for more careful reading those aspects of your background that relate most closely to her needs. In this regard the layout of your resume—typeface and font selection, use of white space, and placement of content—becomes as important as the content itself.

The form supplied earlier for the preparation of your Summary can just as well be used to catalog your full arsenal of Experience. Just be sure all promotions and increased responsibilities are logged in to give readers the best possible sense of your professional growth and stability. Again, tie accomplishments to tangible problems solved, action *you* took (if you shared it, say so), and results achieved from this action—quantified where you can.

Other Personal Data

Education

Start with your most advanced degree. List the name and location of your school, your major, and the year you graduated. (Exception: Those of you 45 years old or more might consider being more circumspect if you think your age is working against you—meaning, don't use dates before a preassigned point.) Include any scholarships and honors you received, as well as your grade point average, if it was notable. (Exception: Those of you 10 years or more out of school will want to put less emphasis on the Education entry. The older you are the less relevant this section becomes.)

List any career-related extracurricular activities, and all career-related, not-for-credit courses and professional seminars you've completed, regardless of whether the company paid for them. Include all licenses and certifications that are even remotely career-related.

Miscellaneous Entries

Some other entries often seen on resumes belong here. Others either waste space or work against you. One in particular is worth special attention:

- Career-related hobbies—Yes

NOTE: For some positions, consider including those hobbies that add a healthy element of risk-taking to your profile (such as a pilot's license); or a thirst for vigorous activity, indicating a high-energy level (for example, mountain climbing or a SCUBA certification).

Don't underestimate the impact some of this information may have in beginning a bonding process between you and one or more of your company interviewers. Aside from your professional qualifications for the job, interviewers (particularly those who would work with you on a regular basis) will be looking for a co-worker with whom there is a potential for some compatibility. Shared interests are one good source.

- Military—Yes; emphasize career-related assignments (also, for the reason noted above: "Yo—Semper Fi!")
- Marital status; weight; height; number and ages of children—No
- Level of computer literacy—Yes, if career-related, including appropriate specifics
- State of health—No ("Excellent" is the only word ever used, anyway)
- Foreign language facility—Yes, if career-related
- Photograph—No
- "References available on request"—No (when they're needed, you'll be asked for them)

- Letters of recommendation—No (they're usually from a previous employer feeling guilty about termination or downsizing)
- Separate lists of "Selected Professional Accomplishments" (often a valuable "leave-behind," particularly for a sales or marketing specialist)

Final Assembly

Now it's time to put it all together. Don't be alarmed if your first complete draft runs three or four pages. Better to have to cut than strain to come up with enough about yourself to fill a single page.

Eliminate all duplications and overlaps. Check for consistency in style and usage. If you don't have a computer Spellcheck, find a human one. Ask a professional colleague to check what you've written to see if you've forgotten anything or have over, under, or misstated any of your good deeds. Appendix F lists a number of action verbs you might find useful.

If your final version runs to a page and a third or a page and a half, don't pad it to fill the entire second page, unless you decide that the entire document could use a bit more white space or wider margins. For overall appearance, check with a friend whose eye you trust if your own is suspect.

Before you decide on paper or printing format, check the resumes of several friends and pick one you like—or maybe parts from two or more that you like. (See also the samples on pages 68–91.) Choose a typeface that is both dignified and easy to read, avoiding any styles that draw attention away from the content itself.

Collecting reactions and suggestions regarding your resume can be the source for another kind of assistance. In explaining why you are changing jobs and what you are looking for, you may find that your "advisor" has ideas for *where* you might be looking, as well. This is one basis for "networking," described in detail in Chapter 4.

A MASTER COVER LETTER

No two cover letters will be the same, because no two sets of job circumstances will be the same. Nevertheless, you need a basic cover letter from which to create the numerous individual responses to the opportunities you generate during the job search. For example, you'll need letters for:

- Proposals to corporations or institutions (usually following a telephone introduction)
- Introductions to executive recruiters or employment agencies
- "Cold calls" to announce a slight career change
- Responses to newspaper or trade journal ads
- "I'm-back-in-the-job-market" reintroductions.

We'll take up some of these situations in detail in Chapter 4, and others later in the second book, *Conquer Interview Objections*. But first a few words about basic cover-letter components. The cover letter gives you the opportunity to introduce yourself in human terms, neutralizing the impersonally written resume. It is also a chance to more comprehensively address specific job requirements and your ability to meet them—improving your chances, one hopes, for the interview that will allow you to take the process a step further.

Except for blind ads (in which the hiring company is not identified), no cover letter should be sent without including the name and correct title of the addressee. "To whom it may concern" letters get thrown out immediately. So do letters sent to functional titles, unless by complete chance a quick scan of your resume discloses a perfect match for an open position.

This is to say that "broadcast letters," or mailings to large numbers of companies in the hope that an opportunity exists—but with no such specific knowledge—are largely a waste of time, paper, and postage. Employers on the receiving end regard such mailings as desperation measures, which in many instances is the case. Many executives and human resource professionals dismiss the senders out of hand for their presumption that a company would be interested in them when they obviously know little more about it than the correct street address.

One excellent model for a basic cover letter goes back at least to 1929. In "Little Blue Book No. 1340," *How to Get a Job*, author Heinz Norden encouraged job seekers to use the four elements of a good sales call to guarantee success in their job campaigns. These four elements were: Command Attention, Sustain Interest, Assure Con-

viction, and Incite Action. They work as well today as they did back
then. Here's how:

Attention

Because there is so much competition for readership, business letters need to scream in some way to assure that the rest of the letter
gets read. This needn't be gimmicky. In fact, gimmicks are a turn-
off to a lot of people, and you can't be sure you know your reader
well enough to use one, even if you're good at it.

Sometimes simply stating your business in a powerful and
straightforward way will work. Always put the reader's needs first.
You might rely on a news peg—perhaps a new product line an-
nounced by the target company, or an earnings increase, an acquisition, or a quote from the company president's recent interview.

Interest and Conviction

These two paragraphs (or sections) can be considered interchange-
able because there is enough built-in flexibility to allow a variety of
presentations. Most important is to *put forth your credentials in terms
of the job's requirements* (don't forget quantifiable accomplishments)
in terms that will indeed sustain interest and assure conviction.

Action

A good cover letter needs to move the reader to action. In most
instances you're looking for an interview, and shouldn't be bashful
about asking for one. To drive home the point, let the reader know
that you'll be calling to see when such an interview might be
scheduled. A reader who knows a call is coming is more likely to
keep your existence in mind, even if she views you as an irritant. At
least you won't be doomed to a bottom-of-the-In-Box non-decision.

Here is a form that will help you write your master cover letter:

1. Write and refine two or three ways you might capture the
   reader's **attention**. *Hint:* Keep in mind the prospective
   employer's *requirements.*

   a. _____

   _____

   _____

b. _____

_____

_____

2. Why should the reader be **interested** in you? What can you do to fill the job's requirements? *Hint:* Emphasize your strengths. Use strong action verbs (see Appendix F). Demonstrate your ability to fill the employer's needs.

a. _____

_____

b. _____

_____

c. _____

_____

_____

3. **Convince** your reader that you should come under strong consideration for the job. *Hint:* Tailor your accomplishments for each position sought. Make them fit the situation at hand.

a. _____

_____

_____

b. _____

_____

_____

c. _____

_____

_____

4. Ask your reader for the interview, or any other **action** you want her to take. *Hint:* Don't leave the decision in the employer's hands.

a. _____

_____

_____

b. _____

_____

_____

Refine all of your responses until they ring true and fully express your intent. Then put them together in letter form, and ask a friend or your mate to critique it.

Get the Flab Out

In your final edit, eliminate all weak words and expressions. Make every word count in your cover letters, just as you did in your resume. Here are some words that will take the punch out of any cover letter and dilute your message accordingly, adapted from *Four Steps to Better Business*, published by Brown House Communications:[1]

"Quite" (I quite agree.)

"Rather" (It was rather disappointing.)

"Indeed" (We are indeed grateful.)

"Frankly" (Frankly, I'm puzzled.)

"A bit" (He's a bit upset.)

"Overall" (Overall, I feel much better.)

"Largely" (My background is largely in exporting.)

Also look closely at sentences that may be flabby. Here are a few, with suggested replacements:

BAD:　　"Enclosed herewith find a copy of my resume."

BETTER:　"Enclosed is my resume."

BAD:　　"It certainly was a pleasure speaking with you on the telephone today, especially so in learning that the position we discussed is one that I might admirably fill."

---

[1]Brown House Communications, P.O. Box 536, Wilton, CT 06897.

> **BETTER:** "Thanks for your time on the phone today. I'll call next week to see when we can meet about the cherry picker opening."
>
> **BAD:** "I believe that the utilization of my marketing skills and accomplishments will result in an impressive profit contribution for your company."
>
> **BETTER:** "My marketing skills and accomplishments match your needs in the following three ways:"

Finally, here are a few buzzwords sure to introduce a fatal element of phoniness to your presentation:

"Interface" (A computer term best left in the computer world.)

"Impact" (Fine as a noun, but avoid using it as a verb—for example, as in "impacting" your present employer's bottom line.)

"Communicate" (Not to be used as a substitute for "talk," "write," or "speak." Example: "I will be happy to communicate my ideas at your convenience.")

"Indicate" (an inferior substitute for "said," as in "Last time we met, you indicated . . . ")

The two examples on pages 165–166 should make it easy for you to distinguish between a good and a bad cover letter. (If not, maybe we failed to get the flab out of the preceding section.) Additional letter samples, with commentary, can be found in Chapter 4 as they relate to your marketing plan, and in conjunction with specific job searches in Chapter 5 of *Conquer Interview Objections*.[2]

THE FLEXIBLE RESUME

Now you have your resume and cover letter templates. If the final version is on your word processor or personal computer, keep a backup on file so that a version of your original is available for reference. In another file save sentences, phrases, or complete entries that didn't make the final cut. Some of these may be useful in another situation.

---

[2]Names and addresses on all resumes and letters reproduced in this book have been changed to protect the identities of both authors and addressees.

CHARLOTTE W. KRUSE
124 Brown Street
West Chicago, Illinois   60141
(708) 414-3871

July 16, 1994

Mr. Robert J.R. Fillett
First National Text House
1010 W. Madison Street
Chicago, IL   60016

Dear Mr. Fillett:

Earlier this week I had the opportunity to speak with Art Farmer, your National
Sales Director, who told me a little about the Executive Editor's opening in your
Adult Education department.   This position interests me very much, and I believe
my background would enable me to contribute significantly to the department's
success. According to Art, there are three aspects of this position on which you
place a high priority.   Let me address them one by one:

Requirements	My Qualifications
Strong management background in the educational publishing industry	Nine years with a $70MM publisher of educational materials in a variety of managerial roles, including Manager of Long-Range Planning, Editor-in-Chief, and Managing Editor.
Strategic planning	Developed a publishing strategy for the science math, language arts and social studies departments increasing sales from $17.6MM to $69.5MM. Programs included ESL components and provisions for low-level students. As Managing Editor, my publishing strategy increased sales from $1.8M to $9.6MM.
Staff development	Hired/trained managers and staff capable in all phases of product development, assuring that quality product was produced on schedule and to budget.

I welcome an opportunity to discuss this position with you in more detail. I'll call
next week to see if you agree that mutual interest might be served by a meeting.

Sincerely,

Charlotte W. Kruse

```
Dear Sir or Madam:


I am responding to your advertisement in _____.


Enclosed please find my resume for your consideration. As my resume

indicates, I have extensive experience in _____, as

well as _____. I would welcome the opportunity

to meet with you at your earliest convenience.


Yours truly,




_____
Harold O. Sweet
```

Invest in a supply of the paper of your choice for printing out different versions of your resume. It's acceptable for executive recruiters to send resume copies to clients, but when candidates make presentations to companies on their own, appearance counts much more. (Consider overprinting the name, address, and phone number portion of your resume as a letterhead for accompanying letters.)

What to Change?

Most new resume situations will simply call for a change of Objective. The next largest number will call for a change of both Objective and Summary. The way the job is structured may necessitate a resequencing of your Summary statement, or perhaps adding or deleting one or two entries. (For examples, see Chapter 5.)

Far less frequently will you need to tinker with the Experience entries, unless an accomplishment you saved and did not use turns out to be one of the top three or four job specs, as determined by your research of the company. If that's the case, you'll want to add it to the Summary as well. Those of you with dual career paths, of course, will need two quite different resumes. And a final, sizable number of you won't need to tinker with your resume at all if you simply want a better job in a field or function you enjoy and want to stay in. (Examples of these, in various professions, appear following Chapter 3.)

We'll get to specific before-and-after examples in Chapter 5, as you begin to execute your individualized marketing plan and learn how to overcome whatever resume objections are plaguing you. But first, let's put a marketing plan together.

SAMPLE RESUMES

The resumes on the following pages have been selected from a number of industries, levels, and functions. If you don't see yourself through these three categories, it could be worth your while to read through the resumes anyway. You may discover a phrase you can use, or perhaps a way of expressing an accomplishment that you can apply to your own situation.

Although these resumes were typed or typeset on $8^1/2$" x 11" paper originally, it was necessary to reduce them to fit this book's trim size of 6" x 9". Two unfortunate consequences are the result:

First of all, the different ratios work against each other. The 6" x 9" page is longer and skinnier than a shape measuring $8^1/2$" x 11". This means that in shrinking the resumes, more space appears at the bottom of our pages than was the case on the originals.

Second, any page reduction obviously means reduced type size, as well. The result with one of the typefaces used has caused some letters to fill in slightly on several of the resumes.

We hope you will bear with us for inadvertently violating two of the Appearance and Clarity principles described on pages 48 and 49.

HELEN SMEDBERG * 2345 KANSAS AVENUE * NEW ROCHELLE, NY 10801 * (914) 468-9871

OBJECTIVE: **SALES/SALES MANAGEMENT**
Challenging sales/marketing position with potential for growth to management level

SUMMARY: Five years experience in developing sales and marketing campaigns for EDP hardware and software in diverse general territory. Developed expertise in pinpointing and designing solutions to client problems. Created innovative individualized proposals and field presentations. Demonstrated ability to exceed quota and close key sales. Developed skills adaptable to related situations requiring conceptual or intangible setting.

EXPERIENCE:

1989 to
Present

XEROX CORPORATION, Mineola, NY
Associate Marketing Representative

Personal responsibility for sales and service to eight major accounts accounting for revenue of approximately $350,000/year

* Conducted product demonstrations and described benefits to executive level client representatives

* Attained 132% of quota in 1987

* Qualified for 100% Club during each year of eligibility

* Presently upgrading three accounts with sales of more than $100 million to current hardware and software lines

* Received awards for new account development in competitive market

* Developed detailed data presentations for Cost/Benefit analyses in conjunction with proposals and presentations

* Maintained high visibility and communication with accounts as liaison between client and IBM personnel

* Developed specialization in manufacturing and distribution accounts

* Received two years of in-depth IBM training; acquired wide-ranging business background in computer applications and problem solving techniques

* Organized seminars/education programs on behalf of clients

* Coordinated multiple details during pre- and post-installation periods

PROFESSIONAL EDUCATION:

XEROX, San Jose, CA
Manufacturing Industry and Applications

XEROX, Poughkeepsie, NY
Distribution and Wholesale Industry and Applications

XEROX, New York, NY
Financial Marketing Analysis

EDUCATION:

Pace University, Pleasantville, NY
BA - Psychology, 1989

Pace University, Pleasantville, NY
MA - Marketing (candidate)

68

SANDRA SELLECK   102 Northshore, Cranston, PA   19543

OBJECTIVE: Public Relations/Corporate Communications

**CAREER
HIGHLIGHTS:**

1991 to Present	**Regal Publications, Inc., New York, NY** Director of Publicity

* Conceive and follow through on promotional campaigns for major books

* Place publicity in national publications; set author interviews on radio and TV; negotiate store tie-ins

   -- First full-length Regal review in New York Times; national recognition of Regal

   -- Special in-store displays at FAO Schwarz and Lord & Taylor

* Constantly develop reviewer lists

* Work closely with editorial and sales

* Author Allan Gibbs: "Absolutely fabulous publicity"

1989 to 1991	**American Federation of Television and Radio Artists, New York, NY** Committees Coordinator

* Established committees of varied segments of membership successfully attained positive communication

   -- Maintained liaison between local members and executive staff and between AFTRA and "outside" influences

* Worked with highly confidential information

1988 to 1989	**District Council 37, Education Department, New York, NY** Writer/Administrative Assistant

* Publicized courses offered by Council to its members; coordinated with educational institutions relative to scheduling and registration

* Wrote and published course handbook (became standard literature for department)

1985 to 1988	**McGraw-Hill, Inc., New York, NY** Associate Director of Publicity

* Wrote/designed publicity/sales promotional material; selected and placed visuals

   -- Increased press coverage/sales through copy acclaimed by reviewers and authors

* Booked authors on network and local television and radio shows

69

1982 to   **Schrimer Books, New York, NY**
1988   Freelance Editor

         * Handled all editorial production for this division of Macmillan Company from manuscript to blues

         * Sig Norton, Publisher: "You saved my life."

1980 to   **Angram Records, New York, NY**
1982   Director of Publicity, Classical Division

         * Brought relatively unknown label to attention of national music media

           -- First complete recording of Berlioz' Les Troyens named "Recording of the Year" for 1981

         * Set up interviews with newspapers and magazines, appearances on radio and TV for recording artists; promoted open recording sessions and parties

         * Maintained still-existing liaison with press agents, reviewers, radio stations

1978 to   **Baltimore National Symphony, Washington, DC**
1980   Editor, Program Book

         * Wrote 95% of program notes for concert repertoire and laid out weekly program book published for concert audiences

         * Maintained liaison between printer and concert office

1977 to   **The History Book Club, New York, NY**
1978   Assistant Editor

         * Read hardcovers and manuscripts for potential paperback publication

         * Wrote cover copy

         * Put together two anthologies: opera, vampire literature

EDUCATION: Columbia University, New York, NY
                  1975-MA, Music/English

                  New York University, New York, NY
                  1973-BA

**SCHOOL
ACTIVITIES:** Represented Music Department at Long Island Contemporary Arts Festival
                  Worked on college newspaper and literary magazine
                  Participated in symphony orchestra and chorus

LANGUAGES: Read, speak and translate German

MARGARET MELGOSA

32 West 12th Street
Apt. 14G
New York, NY   10015

Telephone Numbers:
(212) 866-9814
(212) 483-1481

OBJECTIVE: PORTFOLIO MANAGER/FINANCIAL MANAGEMENT

SUMMARY:

- Three years' experience as an aggressive, sales-oriented brokerage house account executive

- Creative securities manager in developing options trading strategies in profitable customer service activity

- Thorough and definitive researcher of market viability as a whole and of individual stocks

- Bilingual: English-Spanish

BUSINESS HIGHLIGHTS:

1983 to Present   MOORE & SCHLEY, CAMERON & CO., New York, NY
Account Executive

* Initiate research and development of options trading strategy for list of 50 clients; advise on covered writing

* Develop special portfolio strategies for individual customers

* Inaugurated advertising campaign in Hispanic media; doubled market in Latin community from 100 to 200 clients ($60,000 in earnings)

* Successfully develop strong leads from general advertising with 20% conversion to sales

* Redesigned brokers' desks for maximum utility at minimum cost

1982 to 1983   MERRILL, LYNCH, PIERCE, FENNER & SMITH, New York, NY
Account Executive

* Promoted to account executive after short training period; charged with writing options trading strategy for account executives

-- Completed training program in least time of any trainee

EDUCATION: Columbia University, Graduate School of Business
1982 - MBA, Finance/Accounting

Columbia University, Graduate School of Arts and Sciences
1980 - graduate study, Mathematical Sociology
President, Columbia Pine Society

University of Mexico
1974 - BA, Sociology/Economics

OTHER EXPERIENCE (in Mexico):

1975 - 77   AGRO MEXICO - Supervisor, Traffic Department

1972 - 74   ACADEMIA MEXICANA - Quantitative analysis of population survey
of Mexico

1970 - 77   MEXICO CITY DAILY NEWS - Frequent analysis of foreign press
articles

RUTH JOHNSON
2 Sentry Place
French Lick, IN
(219) 472-3206

SUMMARY

A high energy, customer-oriented and results-driven marketing executive with broad experience. Expertise in developing and implementing marketing programs to gain a competitive edge and improve market penetration. A team-building leader with strong project management, innovative problem solving, analysis, formal presentation and communication skills.

CAREER HISTORY AND ACCOMPLISHMENTS

PARODY SERVICES COMPANY, Indianapolis, IN
Account Manager, Client Sales and Marketing (1993-Present)

* Generated $1.75 million in revenue
* Increased revenue contribution of key accounts by an average of 50% within one year
* Provided consultative marketing services to both Fortune 500 and start-up firms, including Compaq, Symantec's Peter Norton Group, Dreyfus, Dean Witter, Discover Card and Softdisk Publishing
* Pioneered new application, which increased client's sales by 90% within first quarter
* Focused on account retention and growth through strategic planning, project management, forecasting and analysis
* Developed and presented renewal and multi-faced promotion plans
* Staged formal presentations to client Senior Management to report marketing successes and future opportunities
* Successfully negotiated contracts

Account Executive, Merchandise Marketing (1992-1993)

* Generated $500,000 in revenue resulting in a 60% increase over the prior year
* Launched the most successful new merchandise client introduction in company history
* Increased response rates for key accounts by 15%
* Maintained and expanded national online retail accounts including Baxter Computer Centers, Fox Camera, Sale Hunter, Luden's and Summerston Utilities
* Managed creative staff to ensure that online projects were completed effectively and expediently
* Identified marketing improvement opportunities and presented formal findings to clients and management

Product Developer, Banking, Finance & Grocery (1991-1992)

* Translated marketing objectives into successful creative executions
* Designed innovative online applications for clients such as First National Trust, Great Eastern Bank, Huntington's Bank, D'Angelico's Supermarket and Red Dog Supermarket
* Acted as project manager to ensure that creative team met project objectives and deliverables
* Led award-winning Quality Task Force. Reduced campaign creation time frames from 12 to eight weeks, improved the quality of the work created and enhanced interdepartmental relationships

DINER'S CLUB COMPANY, New York, NY
Business Analyst, Worldwide Quality Assurance (1986-1991)

* Served as internal consultant to 26 markets worldwide
* Critiqued and improved the quality of customer service to international Diner's Club cardholders in international markets
* Performed operational quality audits in Canada, England and Italy and presented findings to senior management
* Wrote, and managed staff to produce worldwide senior management report

73

EDUCATION

Cornell University, Ithaca, New York
   Bachelor of Science, May 1986

Awards:
* Parody Citation for Quality
* First Annual Parody President's Quality Award

Professional Affiliations:
* Alumni Class Officer: Cornell Fund Representative
* National Association of Female Executives

KARA SIOBHAN KENNEDY

418 Spring Road
Batavia,IL   60130
(708) 484-5667

**CAREER
OBJECTIVE**

To obtain an entry-level position in the social services
field which will enable me to utilize my sociology knowledge
and experience.

EDUCATION

1990-94

Antioch College, Yellow Springs, Ohio
Bachelor of Arts, May 1994

- Major: Sociology/Anthropology
- Minor: History
- GPA: 3.16/4.0
- Major GPA: 3.5/4.0

Summer 1992

Trinity College, Dublin, Ireland

EXPERIENCE

Summer 1993

Family Services, Aurora Superior Court, Aurora IL
Judicial Intern   State of Illinois Judicial Department

- Worked closely with Family Services' counselors throughout
  the judicial process.
- Managed a caseload of direct client services and
  participated in mediation.
- Processed domestic violence cases.

Summer 1992

Trinity College, Dublin, Ireland
Semester in Ireland

- Studied Irish families compared to American families.
- Studied gender roles and relations in Irish culture.

Summer 1991

Morse Moving, North American Van Lines, Geneva, IL
Moving Assistant

- Organized and arranged customer's belongings for moving.
- Established and maintained rapport with customers.

Summer 1990

Xerographics, St. Charles, IL
Operations Assistant

- Prepared duplications of customer documents.
- Established pricing and credit for customer services.

ACTIVITIES

1990 - 1994

Kappa Alpha Theta Fraternity, Yellow Springs, OH

- Purchasing Officer
- Standards Committee

HONORS

National Dean's List Recipient
Alpha Kappa Delta - Sociology Honor Society
Phi Alpha Theta   - History Honor Society

1992-94

Panhel Recipient for Scholarship Merit

REFERENCES

Furnished upon request from the Antioch Career Planning and
Placement Office, 324 Hamilton Williams Center, Yellow
Springs, OH 43049 Tel: (614) 398-3165.

John A. Ellis

Florida State U. Box 421
Tallahassee, FL   02145
(218) 555-3214

L197 Walden Circle
Orlando, FL 02185
(218) 555-9875

Objective: To obtain a position in Corporate Finance.

Education: Florida State University   Tallahassee, FL
                  Bachelor of Science   May 1994
                  Majors: Economics and Finance   GPA 3.0

Achievements: Elected Blue Key National Honor Society member, Spring 1991.
                  Financed 50% of college tuition and 100% of educational expenses.

Experience: Theta Chi Fraternity   Florida State University
                  President   1993
                  * Developed interpersonal, organizational, and leadership skills.
                  * Planned and presided in all chapter meetings.
                  * Interacted regularly with administrators and student government officials.
                  * Educated and prepared pledges for leadership on campus and in society.
                  * Negotiated and implemented fiscal budget for eight executive officers.
                  * Recipient of scholarship to Chapter Leadership Conference: Chapel Hill, N.C.
                  * Achieved $5000 goal for three annual charities: United Way, Oxfam, and Red Cross
                  * Dedicated more than 20 hours per week.

                  Tallahassee Bank of Commerce   Tallahassee, FL
                  Consultant   Fall 1993
                  * Analyzed and recommended feasibility of new branch for $57M bank with MCFE group.
                  * Developed industry outlook through research at Federal Reserve.
                  * Performed financial forecasts and break-even analysis for proposed branch.
                  * Analyzed current financial position to support decision.
                  * Formulated competitive strategy and presented proposal to bank officials.
                  * Utilized and strengthened quantitative and qualitative skills.

                  "It's About Time"   Provincetown, MA
                  Store Manager/Founder   Summers 1992-94
                  * Managed all aspects of retail watch store.
                  * Designed efficient financial record-keeping to monitor cash and credit accounts.
                  * Improved 1500-unit merchandise supply.
                  * Increased sales more than 24% above last year's totals.
                  * Formulated and implemented innovative marketing strategy to outperform competition.
                  * Motivated, trained and supervised staff to meet daily and weekly sales goals.
                  * Dedicated more than 70 hours per week.

                  Florida State University   Tallahassee, FL
                  Resident Assistant   Sept. 1993-Present
                  * Advised 80 residents on academic, social and personal issues.
                  * Promoted student development and campus involvement.
                  * Fostered a greater understanding of community and student diversity.
                  * Enforced college policies and encouraged student responsibility.
                  * Planned and initiated social and academic programs.
                  * Acted as liaison between college administration and students.

Computer: Lotus 1-2-3, Microsoft Word, Harvard Graphics, Lindo.

Personal: Enjoy skiing, golf, tennis, and travel

FORTUNA KOOKY

8118 Alabaster Avenue, Des Moines, IA (515) 414-3181

PROFESSIONAL SUMMARY

Currently employed as an editor in the business section of the *Chicago Bugle* and have worked for four other dailies, including the *Cleveland News*, where I was an Assistant City Editor.

Experienced in all aspects of the business, including rewrite, copy desk, layout and makeup. As a reporter I have covered both police beat and city hall, worked general assignment and written in-depth personality profiles. Familiar with latest newsroom electronic equipment.

EMPLOYMENT

CHICAGO BUGLE. ASSISTANT EDITOR, Op-Ed Page and Business, 1987-present
Extensive experience editing copy, writing headlines, rewriting copy, laying out pages, closing pages in the composing room.

CLEVELAND NEWS. *ASSISTANT CITY EDITOR*, 1981 - 1987
At various times:
Night State Editor, with responsibility for state house bureau, politics writer, large network of state stringers.
Weekend City Editor, with responsibility for entire city room operation.
Assistant Metro Editor, second in command of suburban operation including four zoned editions with staff of 18 reporters, 4 photographers and full copy desk.
City Hall Reporter

CLEVELAND PLAIN DEALER. *ASSISTANT NEWSFEATURE EDITOR.* 1978-1981
Responsible for daily columnists and Sunday People Page. Wrote daily People Page. Wrote or purchased regularly featured in-depth personality profiles. Also involved as an editor in the start-up of Knight-Ridder wire service.

ROANOKE STAR LEDGER. *NEWS COPY DESK.* 1978

RICHMOND HERALD STATESMAN. *REPORTER.* 1975-1978.

EDUCATION

University of California, Berkeley. B.A. Criminology and English.
Graduate Courses: Columbia University, NYC
                        New School for Social Research, NYC
                        Alliance Francais, Paris

NELSON I. BEERS
Lentz Trail, Jim Thorpe, PA   18229
Work: (717) 325-2625   Home: (717) 325-4106

SUMMARY:

Skilled, hands-on, multi-talented business and litigation attorney with significant experience in labor and employment litigation and legal matters affecting corporations. Globally-oriented lawyer with experience in international business community. Entrepreneurial, creative and well-organized manager with solid business instincts.

PROFESSIONAL EXPERIENCE:

PRIVATE LAW PRACTICE, Pennsylvania and New York   1993-Present
Selected representation of corporate clients in corporate, employment and litigation matters while serving as University General Counsel and as counsel to European law firm on international business transactions and litigation matters.

DREXEL AUTO CORPORATION, Akron, Ohio   1990-1993
Largest operating unit of leading worldwide auto manufacturer with annual revenues of $700 million.

<u>VICE PRESIDENT AND GENERAL COUNSEL</u> reporting to President

Chief Legal Officer for U.S. auto operations and legal liaison with World Headquarters Legal Staff in Geneva, Switzerland

<u>MAJOR ACCOMPLISHMENTS</u>

*   Established legal department from ground up with budget of $1.7 million

*   Coordinated and directed merger and reorganization of U.S. auto operations.

*   Established first environmental policy and program including comprehensive facility and disposal site audit.

*   Established in-house product liability defense team that took over management of all product liability cases and reduced pending cases by 50% with the lowest loss ratio in the U.S. auto industry.

*   Established preventive program for legal review of all contracts, leases, intellectual property filings, document retention,antitrust compliance, marketing materials, warranties and consignment program.

ARTHUR FARSON, P.C., Dayton, OH   1987-1990
Established successful and profitable national labor and employment law practice representing management side.

LYNCH, TUBE, KEEFE & HAIL, South Bend, IN   1981-1987
Associate, then Partner, in 10-attorney trial firm; built labor practice to one third of firm revenues

CRUMWELL AND LOCKWOOD, Geneva, IL   1979-1981
Associate Attorney

78

BAR ADMISSIONS:

Pennsylvania, Florida, District of Columbia
Second, Sixth, Eleventh and D.C. Courts of Appeal
Pennsylvania and Arkansas Federal District Courts
U.S. Supreme Court

EDUCATION:

YALE LAW SCHOOL, J.D., 1979
UNIVERSITY OF ALASKA, B.A. 1976 (Summa Cum Laude)

PROFESSIONAL ASSOCIATIONS:

Chairman, Export Trade Committee and Member of International Business Law
Committee of the American Bar Association

Member of Product Liability Law Committee of the American Bar Association

Member of the Corporate Bar Association (Litigation and Insurance Committee)

Member of American Corporate Counsel Association (Vice-Chair, International
Legal Affairs Committee)

PUBLICATIONS:

Co-author, Working with Environmental Consultants, John Wiley, 1994

Counseling Foreign Owned Corporations, 10 Preventive Law Reporter 1, March
1993

Pennsylvania Lawyers Basic Practice Manual, Labor Law Section, 1985

Theft of Business Opportunity, 53 Pennsylvania Bar Journal 2, 1991

Joinder of Claims, Parties and Counterclaims, 51 Pennsylvania Bar Journal 4,
1979

OTHER ACTIVITIES:

University of Alaska
1993 Recipient of Distinguished Alumnus Award; Past Member of Board of
Governors and Executive Committee; Presidential Search Committee; Past President
of Alumni Association; Adjunct Professor of Law, Economics and Management
Science

The Philadelphia Graduate Center of Rensselaer Polytechnic Institute
Adjunct Professor of Management

Clifford W. Beers Guidance Clinic
Past Member Board of Directors

Town of Madison Economic Development Commission
Past Member and Chairman

Gene Jaeger

903 S. Country Club Road
Mesa, AZ 85713

Bus: (602) 319-2780
Res: (602) 595-0641

Summary

More than 10 years experience in human resources field with a strong international and domestic background in compensation planning, development and administration.

Experience

Knight-Ridder Newspapers, Inc., Miami, FL   1993-Present

International Personnel Manager

Direct administration of all personnel policies and programs for more than 300 overseas employees in 33 locations. Manage three-person department with a $750,000 annual budget.

* Developed international compensation and benefit policies for 140 U.S. expatriate employees.

* Implemented overseas allowance policy and tax equalization program for U.S. expatriate and third-country national employees.

* Established local payroll systems and benefit plans for more than 100 local national employees in Europe and the Far EAst.

* Managed all international relocations.

General Mills, Inc., Minneapolis, MN   1990-93

Associate Personnel Manager

Provided personnel generalist for Beverage and Breakfast Food Divisions (combined revenues over one billion dollars).

* Administered corporate compensation and benefit programs and policies for all exempt and non-exempt headquarters personnel.

* Implemented human resource succession plans for both Divisions.

* Developed successful Affirmative Action PLan and EEO Procedures.

* Planned and executed MBA recruiting program on an annual basis.

Digital Equipment Corp., Enfield, CT   1988-90

Senior Consultant

* Managed and executed compensation assignments for a variety of clients in both public and private sectors.

Anheuser-Busch Companies Inc., St. Louis, MO   1987-88

Compensation Analyst

National Recruiting Coordinator

Deutsche Bank, AG, Frankfort/Main, Germany   1988-87

Personnel Assistant to Managing Director

Education

Duke University, Durham, NC, MBA   1984
Duke University, Durham, NC, BA   1982

   Elected to Phi Beta Kappa

Additional Information

Faculty member of American Compensation Association; currently teaching course in International Compensation. Speaker on international compensation at Conference Board and American Management Association meetings in 1992 and 1993.

FRANK CRESSON, 25 NORTHRIDGE ROAD, SUMMIT, NEW JERSEY, 07964
Home: (201) 637-6653   Office: (212) 980-8573

OBJECTIVE: SENIOR MANAGEMENT -- BANKING

SUMMARY: Highly motivated and creative international banker with distinguished service and
                     profitablility record in New York, London, Paris and Amsterdam.

CAREER HIGHLIGHTS:

1983 to   CITICORP INTERNATIONAL
Present   New York, NY

                     Vice-President for Europe, Mideast and Africa
                     New York, NY (December 1986 to Present)

                     - Direct all Edge Act marketing and account service for EMEA-New York
                     - Control demand balances in excess of $75,000,000 and 90% of 40,000-plus monthly
                       transaction volume
                     - As senior credit officer for both parent bank and Edge Act subsidary, govern EMEA-
                       New York exposure
                     - Contributed substantially to design of deposit-based earnings credit system for Islamic
                       clients, offsetting cost of future credit services
                     - Principal force in redesign of accounting and profitability model

                     Vice-President and Representative (December 1985 - December 1986)
                     Assistant Vice-President (January 1984 - December 1985)
                     Amsterdam, The Netherlands

                     - Managed corporate and correspondent relationship throughout 23-nation area, coor-
                       dinating efforts with U.S. associates
                     - Directed compilation and analysis of data relative to the economics of developing
                       nations; wrote accceptable business plans accordingly
                     - Met with senior ministers and heads of state throughout Africa, and developed
                       strategies for establishment of credit limits with French West Africa
                     - Designed and implemented special correspondent agreements with compatible
                       European banks, effectively creating a branch network overseas for Citicorp
                     - Consistently surpassed annual goals for deposit gatherings, loan volume, profit-
                       ability and staffing

                     Assistant Vice-President, Corporate Finance
                     London, England (February 1983 - January 1984)
                     - Responsible, as part of team effort, for origination and implementation of new
                       merchant and corporate capabilities for Citicorp in Europe
June 1982   BANK OF AMERICA INTERNATIONAL, LTD.
to   London, England
Jan. 1983   **Manager**
                     - Set up and managed umbrella administration for credit, loan services and syndication
                       areas

Jan. 1980   BANK OF AMERICA INTERNATIONAL S.A. (LUXEMBOURG)
to   Paris, France
June 1982   **Assistant Vice-President and Loan Officer**
                     Banque Ameribas
                     - Member of original team that formed aggressive new merchant bank. Assembled
                       portfolio in excess of $250,000,000 over three-year period, on nominal capital

Sept. 1977   IRVING TRUST COMPANY
to   New York, NY
Jan. 1980   **Assistant Manager**
                     - Coordinated, with treasurers and finance vice-presidents, bridge loans and stock
                       option financing programs for major corporate relationships

82

Oct. 1976 **to** **Sept. 1977**	TRADE BANK AND TRUST COMPANY New York, NY **Assistant Credit Manager**
Feb. 1975 **to** **Sept. 1976**	BANKERS TRUST COMPANY New York, NY **Retail Platform Associate; Branch Operations Supervisor; Collection Clerk; Teller**
EDUCATION:	Columbia University, BA Economics, 1979 University of Geneva (Switzerland), 1970 - Certificate French Language and Civilization Joint Studies Program, Stanford University/Crocker National Bank: Advanced Techniques of Credit and Financial Analysis New York Institute of Credit: Accounting Survey Lecture Series; Credit and the Uniform Commercial Code Lecture Series National Credit Office: Applied Course in Credit and Financial Analysis
LANGUAGES:	Bilingual French-English; read Dutch and Spanish
CITATION:	**Who's Who in the World**
MEMBERSHIPS:	New York Institute of Credit (former) New York Credit and Financial Management Institute (former) American Chamber of Commerce (NL) (present)

JOHN H. WILLIAMSON   1700 York Avenue, Apt. 5B   New York, NY 10021
Office: (212) 249-6625   Home: (212) 249-1523

OBJECTIVE: **ORCHESTRAL CONDUCTOR/CHORAL DIRECTOR**

SUMMARY: More than 15 years as musical director and conductor for symphony
               orchestras, opera companies and university and church chorales. Frequent
               tours of Europe and South America for concert engagements. Possess full
               repertoire of classical and semi-classical scores.

CONDUCTOR: EXPERIENCE
Current   WHITTENBURG CHOIR COLLEGE, Princeton, NJ
               Music Director
               - Conduct University Symphony Orchestra
               - Member, piano faculty
               NATIONAL COUNCIL OF THE ARTS, New York, NY
               - Commissioned to organize Latin-American Symphonic Choir
1980-84   THE MONTAUK ORCHESTRA, Long Island, NY
               - Music Director and Conductor
               FIRST METHODIST CHURCH, Setauket, NY
               - Choral Director with 10-15 concerts per year
1981-83   HOPE OPERA COMPANY, Long Island, NY
               - Orchestral and Choir Director
               - Directed and conducted operatic performances including *I Pagliacci*,
                 Tosca, Magic Flute, and *Cavalleria Rusticana*
1978-80   STATE UNIVERSITY OF NEW YORK AT STONY BROOK, NY
               - Served as Assistant Conductor for four semesters
1970-1973   BUENOS AIRES CONSERVATORY
               - Conductor for orchestra and chorale; piano instructor

TOURING CONDUCTOR:
1980 to   - Guest conductor in South America and Europe (Italy, France, Poland)
                 --Conducted 15 concerts in South America (July/August, 1979)
                   with engagements in Chile, Argentina, Uraguay, Paraguay and
                   Bolivia
INSTRUCTOR:
1979 to   PRIVATE INSTRUCTOR, New York, NY
Present   - Instruct in piano and conducting; coach voice
                 --Currently coaching 15 professional;
                   have coached 60-65 professional
                 --Have instructed more than 120 non-professionals
1975-78   NEW YORK INSTITUTE FOR THE EDUCATION OF THE BLIND, New York, NY
               - Member of the piano faculty
1973-1974   PRIVATE INSTRUCTOR, St. Louis, MO
               - Taught piano and solfege
1969-73   PRIVATE INSTRUCTOR, Buenos Aires, Argentina
               - Taught piano, solfege, ear training and harmony

JUDGE: NEW YORK STATE SYMPHONIC MUSIC ASSOCIATION
               - Annual Spring Festival for entries in piano, chorus and orchestra
               NEW YORK STATE MUSICAL EVALUATION CENTER
               - (First National Competition, 1988-1989)

EDUCATION

DEGREE   STATE UNIVERSITY OF NEW YORK AT STONY BROOK, NY (Full Scholarship)
PROGRAMS: 1980 - MM, Orchestral Conducting/Choral Conducting
              CONSERVATORY NACIONAL OF MUSIC GENERAL URQUIZA, Buenos Aires,
              Argentina (Full Scholarship)
              1973 - PhD, Conducting
              1972 - MM, Music, Orchestral and Choral Conducting
              1969 - BM, Piano/Analysis

ADDITIONAL TRAINING:

              STATE UNIVERSITY OF NEW YORK, Oneonta, NY
              1987 - Seminar in Choral Conducting and Analysis
              MARIANO SIJANEK, Buenos Aires, Argentina
              1985 - Opera Seminar (6 weeks)
              PRIVATE INSTRUCTION, St. Louis, MO
              1972-78 - Orchestral and Choral under professional directors

PROFESSIONAL AFFILIATIONS:

              American Symphony Orchestra League
              Musical Educators National Conference
              Musicians Club
              Piano Teachers of New York

LANGUAGES: Fluent in Spanish, Italian and French; working knowledge of Portuguese
              and German

CITED: *Reader's Digest,* Oct., 1989 (Also published in all 15 foreign language
              editions)
              People Magazine, March 3, 1987
              Various magazine and newspaper articles, U.S. and abroad

DONALD SEIGEL
60 53rd Street
Chicago, Illinois 60614
(312) 673-7321

OBJECTIVE: FINANCIAL ANALYST

SUMMARY: Three years with active and diverse private trust. Emphasis on investment and management of assets. Evaluate investment potential of venture capital situations and going concerns, monitor holdings, troubleshooting assignments. Exposure to financial analysis in many industries and business situations.

EXPERIENCE:
1986 to   A.T.C. COMPANY, Chicago, IL
Present   Asset and Investment Analyst

VENTURE   Evaluate opportunities for equity participation in new ventures; comprehensive
CAPITAL   project analysis; analyze long-run growth and profit potential; recommend action.
PROJECTS

        Example: Recommended financing cosmetics company with innovative pro-
                          duct concept
        Result: Company now making an operating profit on annual sales of over
                          $1,000,000; employs 600 sales personnel in 13 states.
                          (Subsequently appointed to board of directors with full participation
                          in financial planning and policy decisions)

        Example: Advised creation of a company to utilize patented Biophonics
                          technology in greenhouse food production.
        Result: Twenty-five production units now in operation; cost-efficient
                          technology gives company international franchise potential.

REAL ESTATE   Cash flow and R.O.I. analysis, purchase and sale evaluation, pro forma and
ASSIGNMENTS   operating statement preparation, and determination of real estate development
        potential, and troubleshooting.

        Example: On-site in Anchorage, AK, developed turn-around plan for 19 build-
                          ing apartment complex with 55% vacancy rate.
        Result: Improved financial procedures, negotiated financing, repositioned
                          property for the market. Vacancy rate reduced to 40% after only
                          three months; purchase offer under consideration is $1.5 million
                          higher than offer received prior to turn-around plan. (Definitive
                          market survey now used by Anchorage banks)

        Example: Evaluated offer for one of the trust's shopping centers in
                          Pennsylvania
        Result: Analysis utilized in negotiating 29% increase in offer; resulted in
                          sale of the property.

INVESTMENT   Charged with monitoring the performance and security of current holdings and
MANAGEMENT   analyzing other investment opportunities.

        Example: Evaluated acceptability of common stock offered in lieu of note
                          repayment by manufacturer of Pay-TV hardware
        Result: Identified financial weaknesses caused by confused management
                          and marketing efforts; recommended holding the note to secure
                          priority claim on promising technology in case of default or
                          bankruptcy

        Example: Analyzed opportunity to invest in regional operations of national fast
                          food chain.
        Result: Showed profit-margin projections of investor group to be greatly
                          overstated. Prevented potential $700,000 loss.

OTHER ASSIGNMENTS	Acquisition analysis of company engaged in air and ground transport for the entertainment industry
	Monitor and manage securities portfolio
	Negotiate distribution of assets in order to dissolve a corporation
	Evaluation of proposal to develop Florida Cable-TV station
PRIOR EXPERIENCE	Court Liaison for New York County, Court Referral Project, New York, NY Supervised staff of eight (1978-1981)
	Supervisor, Legal Department, Samaritan Halfway Society, Inc., New York, NY Supervised staff of eight (1976-1978)
	High School Graduate Trainee Program, Citibank, New York, NY Trust and Securities Operations (1976-1978)
EDUCATION:	New York University, New York, NY (1/84 - 2/88)

	Jan, 1988 -- BA, Economics/Philosophy
	          Recipient, Arts and Sciences Scholarship
	          Earned 100% living expenses; worked 30 hours per week

	Jan. 1989 -- Candidate for January admission to MBA program at NYU

ELLEN ABRAHMS
4860 Toughy Road
Austin, Texas   78510
612-8450-6695

OBJECTIVE: DIRECTOR OF HUMAN RESOURCES

Personnel Manager with nine years' experience in human resources
administration. Demonstrated ability to work effectively with
employees at diverse levels. Comprehensive knowledge of recruitment,
screening and interviewing; policy implementation; benefits administration;
and staff supervision. Adept at labor negotiations. Innovator with ability to
increase employee morale and improve communications. Experience includes
management, staffing and establishment of personnel procedures for two new
facilities of a major corporation.

PERSONNEL EXPERIENCE:

1985 to   PERMITRON ULTRASONICS, DIVISION OF PERMITRON CORPORATION
Present   Austin, TX
                    Major manufacturer of bio-medical, dental and surgical equipment
                    and industrial applications of ultrasonic technology (union shop with
                    160 employees)

                    Personnel Manager
                    *   Responsible for recruitment, screening and interviewing of exempt, non-
                           exempt and hourly personnel for diversified employment areas
                           - Maintain staffing of technical, electronics, research, medical, production
                              instrument assembly, plant management and general clerical functions

                    *   Also responsible for staffing of Dallas acquisition and new San Antonio
                           facility while handling full personnel management functions in Austin office

                    *   Extensively involved in labor relations, including participation in contract
                           negotiations, adminstration and interpretation of union contract and close
                           interface with union

                    *   Interpret and oversee implementation of all personnel policies; control
                           administration of comprehensive employee benefit programs

                    *   Introduced measure to improve communications and establish employment
                           incentives
                           - Created and issued first policy manual
                           - Established ten-year service award club to promote better relationship
                              between labor and management
                           - Initiated company newspaper

                    *   Establish and maintain EEO guidelines, ensure compliance with federal
                           and state regulations

                    *   Conduct wage and salary analyses to assure competitive compensation
                           position in industry

                    *   Regularly achieve 30% under budget allocation for placement advertising
                           and employment agency commissions

                    *   Supervise three-person department; delegate work flow to 15-person clerical
                           staff

Continued

88

1984-1985   THE SINGER COMPANY, New York, NY
                <u>Assistant, Compensation & Benefits Department</u>
                *   Assistant Director of Compensation & Benefits with office administration;
                     processing of benefit action forms and payroll action forms on terminations,
                     transfers, salary increases and new employees; all related correspondence

                *   Oriented employees relocating overseas regarding cultural, social and
                     psychological adjustments

1978   EQUITABLE LIFE INSURANCE COMPANY, New York, NY
                <u>Adminstrative Assistant</u>
                *   Assisted Director of Group Insurance Department

                *   Tour guide responsible for orientation tours for new employees and visitors

EDUCATION: Queens College, Queens, NY
                Business Major

                1985-Present - Numerous seminars on personnel and management sponsored
                            by AMA and other institutions

PROFESSIONAL AFFILIATIONS:

                International Association of Personnel
                Women Queens Personnel Management Association

ELIZABETH MCBRIDE
221 Midland Avenue
Aiken, South Carolina   29801
(703) 988-0868

SUMMARY

Fourteen years of managerial experience with progressive and increasingly responsible positions in the fields of satellite communications and acquisition.

CAPABILITIES

Acquisitions:
* Develop and prepare solicitations for the procurement of merchandise, equipment, supplies and/or services.
* Analyze and evaluate proposals.
* Perform price/cost analysis.
* Formulate negotiations strategy/conduct negotiations.
* Provide training, guidance and assistance to lower grade specialists.
* Preaward and postaward acquisition functions for 55 contracts valued at more than $47,000,000.

Satellite Communications:
* Develop and prepare applications for FCC licensing of satellite earth stations, microwave stations and experimental stations.
* Calculate and plot station coordinates on maps.
* Sketch site layouts and profiles.
* Prepare notifications to FAA for antenna-supporting tower structures.
* Administering and monitoring functions for more than 200 earth, microwave and experimental station licenses.

EXPERIENCE

CONTRACTS SPECIALIST
Navy Exchange Service Command, NY   1986-Present

ADMINISTRATOR, FCC AUTHORIZATIONS
RCA Frequency Bureau, NJ   1977-1984

PRIOR POSITIONS
Secretarial positions with Navy Exchange Service Command, RCA Frequency Bureau and Metropolitan Life Insurance Company

EDUCATION
College of Staten Island, Staten Island, NY   2 years

New Utrecht High School, Brooklyn, NY, graduate

TRAINING/SELF STUDY

* Defense Small Purchase
* Management of Defense Acquisition Contracts
* Nonappropriated Fund Acquisition Management
* Effective Negotiations
* Supervisory Development
* Supervisory Personnel Administration
* Managing Multiple Priorities
* Time Management
* Introduction to Retailing

ADDITIONAL READING

Boll, Carl R. *Executive Jobs Unlimited*. New York: Macmillan, 1979. Tactics may be a bit dated, but the letter-writing style is worthy of study.

Kine, Julie Adair. *The Smart Woman's Guide to Resumes and Job Hunting*. Hawthorne, NJ: Career Press, 1991. Do's and don'ts; elements and style; cover letters and followup.

Shanahan, William F. *Resumes for Computer Professionals: A Complete Resume Preparation and Job-Getting Guide*. New York: Arco Publishing, Inc., 1983. Samples include resumes for computer sales, repair, engineer, programmer, data processor, analyst, etc.

Strunk, William Jr. and E.B. White. *The Elements of Style*. New York: Macmillan Publishing Company Inc., 1979. The best book available on making words count.

Wilson, Robert F. *Better Resumes for Executives and Professionals (Second Edition)*. Hauppauge, NY: Barron's Educational Series, 1991. Complete information to market oneself for career advancement or change. Includes tips on dealing with job loss; conducting a winning job campaign.

Zinsser, William. *On Writing Well*. New York: HarperCollins Publishers, 1990. In a league with *The Elements of Style* for sound advice on the written word. Dozens of examples of good writing, backed up by sound analysis.

4

Developing an Effective Marketing Plan

Now it's time to implement your new-found organizational and print-related tools.

Presumably by now you have settled on a general direction for your job search (or perhaps on two somewhat similar directions) that you believe will focus your efforts in the months ahead. If your career direction(s) is even slightly different from the work you were doing before you began to read this book, your search strategy will be different from that of a job seeker continuing in the same general arena.

Your task right now, though, is to test whatever premise drives your job search to be sure your energies are aimed at the right targets.

You already know from reading Chapter 1—perhaps as well from your own experience—that the road to your next job will probably not be an easy one. For some time to come the changing economy will adversely affect the job market in ways difficult to predict. All of this means that there are more people than ever competing for the same jobs. Consequently, to compete successfully, you need an edge—some way of standing out from the other candidates in ways that get *you* more job offers. This requires an assertive, pro-active stance, and a thorough, professional approach that leaves nothing to chance.

THE JOB SEEKER AS "PRODUCT"

"Product differentiation" is a method marketing specialists use to gain a competitive advantage in the marketplace. Bottled water is a *differentiated product*—that is, different from tap water, and different (or at least marketed to be so) from every other brand of bottled water sold.

Tap water itself is simply a *commodity*, usually bought from residents' municipal water departments. The demand for bottled water came about in the first place because the quality of tap water fell in so many towns and cities, for various reasons. Even in some areas where tap water quality had not decreased, the bottled water people strongly suggested that consumers would be better off drinking their product instead. Use our differentiated product, they said in effect, rather than the commodity.

Where are we going with this? Most candidates present themselves to potential employers as commodity candidates, rather then attempting to differentiate themselves. Here's an example:

In response to an ad for a planning director, a Chicago consulting firm received more than 300 resumes. One third of the candidates simply put them in envelopes and mailed them. Another third added a cover letter, either referring to the ad or enclosing it. The final third customized their cover letters by including the name and date of the newspaper in which the ad appeared. Ten of these referred to the job by title and summarized their experience accordingly.

Only one applicant organized his letter to reflect the six requirements outlined in the ad, but made no attempt to modify his resume to highlight any of the six requirements. His experience was indeed quite relevant, but the reader had to study the resume to figure it out. As a result, none of these candidates was called in for an interview.

What does this illustrate? Some would say that the newspaper recruitment advertising was ineffective. The vice president and treasurer of the firm, however, analyzed the situation this way:

"I doubt that any one of the candidates gave his response serious consideration. One made a half-hearted attempt, but none seemed sufficiently motivated.

"I thought about this job for months before discussing it with the president. He and I must have traded a half dozen memos before he signed off. Then personnel and I spent more time smoothing out the job specs and carefully wording the ad.

"What is amazing is that 25 of these people telephoned to ask if their resumes had been received and reviewed. They wanted to know if our personnel department had done the analysis for them that they had not been willing to do for themselves.

"I wouldn't want any of these candidates working for me."

With only a little extra effort, a candidate who stood out from these commodity candidates to any extent probably would have been invited in for an interview—and perhaps received a job offer.

In order to differentiate yourself from the commodity candidates, personalize your cover letter for each open position, and reorganize your resume to highlight your competencies in direct relationship to the requirements of the job. You'll be the one in 100 to make this extra effort.

Candidate Features and Benefits

Let's use another sales and marketing analogy, with the job seeker again as our product. Features are the tangible aspects of a product—that one can touch, see, taste, or feel. A feature is the physical reality of the product; the narrative description of the service.

Benefits are the payoff to the prospective buyer; tangible rewards and prospective satisfaction intended to bridge the gap between interest in the product or service and a correlative "need" for it. Let's use two models of a pair of tennis shoes as an example:

Model	Feature	Benefit
ADIDAS Torsion Stefan Edberg	Torsion technology (forefoot and rearfoot move independently)	Improved contact with court; better stability
	Wider toe box and lycra innersleeve	Contoured fit; pain-free play
	High toe bumper	Added protection for toe draggers
CONVERSE React 8500	Encapsulated liquid cushioning	More heel protection and durability
	Ethylene vinyl acetate midsole	Better shock absorbing qualities
	Partial rubber cupsole	Lighter than full rubber cupsole; reduced foot fatigue

As you can see, the days are gone for picking one of the two choices once available—Keds in either white or black canvas—and lacing them above your ankles. Instead we have the world of hi-tech tennis footwear—out there with tens of thousands of other products competing for the attention and dollars of an ever more demanding and conditioned consumer.

Translated to job search, features (from the employer's point of view) are the historical facts surrounding a candidate: the years of schooling, the degrees earned, the grades attained, the jobs held, the budgets managed, the responsibilities handled, the accomplishments achieved, the compensation earned.

Benefits are the payoff for the hiring organization and the hiring manager. They answer these questions:

- What value will you add to their organization?
- What will you do to be worth what they pay you?
- What company or department problems can you solve, both immediately or long-term?
- What can you achieve that nobody else in the organization can?
- What makes you better than all of the other candidates they will interview?

Most candidates make the mistake of selling on the basis of their features rather than their benefits. They spend the greater part of their effort telling an interviewer what they did for other employers, rather than what they can do for the hiring company. By matching your skills to the hiring manager's requirements, you will more easily be seen as able to close that gap between the ideal and the acceptable. A good example is Charlotte Kruse's letter on page 65.

Market Segmentation

Let's take "the job seeker as product" a step further. Product differentiation distinguishes one product from another. "Market segmentation" distinguishes among groups of prospects that may be interested in the product. Once the different groups have been identified, appropriate marketing strategy is developed for each.

For the job seeker, the market segments may be looked at as groups of prospective employers, all representing companies alike in one way but different in others. Job-seeking strategy, after all, includes deciding not only what jobs to pursue, but what jobs *not* to go after as well.

Even if you are between jobs and in need of a paycheck, finding a job simply to *have* a job usually will not be in your best, long-range interests, and may put you in the position of explaining why you lost the last *two* jobs rather than just one. Only you—possibly in collaboration with close friends or family—are in a position to know where to draw your bottom lines, and for what reasons.

Start with what you like and don't like; can stand and can't stand; are and are not willing to put up with. This will give you a checklist you can internalize—and refer to occasionally—so you won't need to give a lot of thought to jobs that, even though attractive, essentially will be a waste of your time. In gray areas where the decision is a difficult one, go for it. You can always back out later, when either a negative part of your first impression is reinforced, or additional downside aspects of the opportunity emerge. Such a course will keep you from attempting to resurrect a job long past filled since you first expressed interest.

Here are some ways of qualifying companies by market segment; in other words, establishing some bottom lines:

• *Industry/Function*—Preparation for a career change—even a slight one—that takes you outside the industry or function you have most recently followed, requires careful planning and positioning. It also requires extensive repackaging of such written credentials as the resumes and cover letters covered in Chapter 3.

When you are considering a target company outside your function or industry, it is essential to make yourself aware of its problems and how you would deal with them—even more so than it would be for a company *within* your specific job area. Your qualifications will be called into question in ways that may surprise you (See Chapter 5 of *Conquer Interview Objections*), so it is essential that you speak with some knowledge of your target company's customers, competitors, and clients, as well as its infrastructure.

• *Geography*—Many people need to psyche themselves to prepare for the workday and unwind on the way home. They don't mind a commute by auto, rail, or bus as their method. Many others want to live near their workplace and spend as little time as possible on the road. (You know who you are.) The way to bottom-line yourself is to pick your own outside commutation limit—whether it's a half hour, an hour, or two hours—and then apply for only those jobs that meet your criterion.

The other element of job selection involving geography is relocation. For any one of a number of reasons, it may be impossible or imprudent for you and your family to consider relocation at this time. An ailing parent or other family member, a real estate market that will turn your house sale into a bloodbath, a spouse's critical paycheck difficult to duplicate in the new location—all could preclude a decision to move for the time being. Before going after a job that is good for you in every respect except geography, draw a bottom line establishing a distance from your current home or office beyond which you will not go—for whatever reason—and stick with your decision until one or more of your circumstances changes.

• *Compensation*—Only you know specifically what trade-offs would cause you to accept a job resulting in a lateral move, or even settling for a slightly lower salary. If you are between jobs, by this time presumably you have examined your financial circumstances closely enough to have formulated action plans. As discussed in Chapter 2, such action plans should be based on finding work over a twelve-month continuum, with interim plans for sieges that last three months, six months, and nine months, as well as for twelve. Cut another way, such data will help you decide just how large your next paycheck must be to meet your short- and long-term obligations.

If you're in doubt as to what the job you want will or should pay, there are a couple of standard reference works you can check out—whether you're working on your first full-time job search, or have been through the exercise before. Most central libraries will have either *The American Almanac of Jobs and Salaries* (Avon) or *American Salaries and Wages Survey* (Gale Research). To zero in more specifically on your industry, periodic wage or salary surveys are published in most trade journals. If you can't find a journal for your industry or function, check the *Business Periodicals Index* (H.W. Wilson). If you are still unsuccessful, call the human resource departments of as many companies likely to have your category of worker in their employ as it takes to get a feeling for the range appropriate to you.

Long-Term Job Prospects

Another perspective that will help is to know where the jobs are likely to be 5 and 10 years from now. A number of experts have illuminated the job market for the end of this century and the beginning of the next. (See also Appendix G: "Where the Jobs Are—and Will Be.")

Carol Kleiman, who writes career-related columns for the *Chicago Tribune*, says positions in health care, engineers of various kinds, and computer-related technical jobs will be in increasing demand. So will such wide-ranging professions as firefighters, chefs, database managers, and astronomers.

In *The 100 Best Jobs for the 1990s and Beyond*, Kleiman identifies health-care needs—from dental hygienists to podiatrists—as "insatiable," driven by an aging population, new technology that keeps people alive longer, the AIDS epidemic, and a growing public awareness of the importance of health care.

Kleiman says computer literacy will be a key skill for landing a growing number of jobs and that the "graying" of the American work force will create labor shortages leading to more opportunities for women, the disabled, minorities, immigrants, and older workers.

Because different experts interpret data in different ways, however—and because their research methods also may differ—don't be discouraged if your field was not singled out in the study described above. It doesn't necessarily mean that career change is your only road to success.

Socio-economic change is a constant, and certainly will signal the promise of career areas other than health care in the years ahead. The way to know this is to keep your antennae out, to spot trends as they begin to emerge. The following section offers a number of suggestions.

Market Research

Whether your intention is to fight or switch, there are a number of ways to help you decide how to narrow your focus among the many possible companies within your market segments. All publicly held companies, for example, are required by the Securities and Exchange Commission to report various kinds of information, all available to the public.

General interest and industry-specific directories.   Dozens of regional, national, and international business directories are available in most public libraries. They contain the information you need—not only for publicly held companies, but for private firms as well. Some of these directories are classified by industry, others by size of company. A selection of both general reference and industry-specific directories appears on pages 116, 118, and 119. If you don't see your specialty listed, ask a local public or university librarian for assistance. Try also *The Directory of Directories,* a research timesaver that will lead you to the directories of most possible assistance to you.

One of the best of the general directories is *The Directory of Corporate Affiliations,* published annually with bimonthly supplements, by the National Register Publishing Company. The DCA lists key data on 5,000 publicly held parent companies—in boldface, to distinguish them (in user-friendly fashion) from their 57,000 respective divisions, subsidiaries, and affiliates. For each of these you'll find inside an address, phone number, business description, stock exchange ticker symbol, annual sales, number of employees, and names of top corporate officers. Additional geographical and Standard Industrial Code (S.I.C.) indexes list all companies by city and state, and primary types of business. Another back-of-the book feature is an index of "corporate responsibility"—a way to find in one place all of the human resource directors, CEOs, treasurers, and purchasing agents, among others. Five annual supplements document significant corporate changes, including acquisitions, mergers, and other dramatic name or status switches. (Additional DCA volumes cover 8,000 private U.S. companies and 33,000 internationally owned companies.)

Other library sources. Joan Silverman, a reference librarian at the New Haven, Connecticut, Free Public Library, points out that much additional career assistance is available in many public libraries. "We have everything a person needs," says Ms. Silverman. "We maintain local, state, and national classifieds, as well as a weekly update of job listings from the State Job Services and civil service listings.

"There are books, directories, and audiovisual materials for specific careers, career changers, and first-time job seekers. The library offers typewriters and computers with resume writing software for public use. A person lucky enough to have an interview can find information about the company. Job seekers looking for *likely* companies can make good use of the same sources." (A complete list of general interest and industry-specific sources appears at the end of the chapter.)

Also check out the special issues of leading business magazines and trade journals for annually updated marketing, sales, and product development information. Finally, ask about recent computer software that calls out references to national companies in business and consumer magazines. One worth looking for is ProQuest, also widely available.

Another good software source is *The Ultimate Job Finder*[1], which offers an annually updated access to 4,500 specialty and trade periodicals, job directories, job matching services, job hotlines, and interactive computer job and resume databases. Just type in your specific profession or job category, and the Job Finder takes it from there. If your library doesn't have it, ask for the books on which it is based, all by David Lauber: *The Professional Job Finder, The Government Job Finder*, and *The Non-Profit Job Finder*.

Take advantage of the full range of job-hunting advice offered at your public library, including discussing your job search with a reference librarian. When they have time, these professionals usually are most willing to help you. If your local library has minimal resources, ask for the location of the nearest larger central or university library at which more extensive resources may be found.

Make it a point to spend at least a half day a week at the best library nearby, if only to browse through current business publications. It's a nice break from specific company research and a good source for fresh job-search ideas. You'll find most industrial trends covered by one or more of the major business magazines (*Fortune, Forbes, Business Week*, etc.) as well as stories of particular interest to job seekers—occasionally tips on the job search itself.

These magazines (as well as regional editions of *The Wall Street Journal*, published daily) regularly report company-level developments in a variety of industries, including related articles and profiles of leading executives. Take notes on companies that interest you, as well as on individuals in them who may become valuable contacts, either now or in the future.

Target company information sources.   Another good way to gather information about hiring companies is from their most recent annual reports, the more financially detailed 10-Ks, or any descriptive literature available from their marketing or public relations departments. These publications offer a full range of information about a company's products and services, including recent projections of

---

[1]Information Products, 887 S. Orem Blvd., Orem, UT 84058.

long-range strategies and objectives. Annual reports and 10-Ks will give you a better notion of a company's financial status and growth strategy. Call the company and tell the operator what you want.

AVENUES TO MARKET

Most new job seekers working out a strategy for putting their marketing program in gear turn first to the want ads. They don't yet realize that relying on print advertising is one of the lower-yield methods of job search.

In 1991, the authors conducted a survey of about 50 Columbia University Business School graduates participating in a job search seminar. They had been out of school from 5 to 25 years, representing most major industries and functions. Many of them had changed jobs one or more times since graduation. We asked them what marketing avenues had been the source of their job leads. Four sources were mentioned most frequently, ranking as follows:

Networking	58 percent
Executive recruitment	16 percent
Print advertising	14 percent
Direct mail	7 percent
Other	5 percent

(A sample comprised of a modest group of Ivy League graduates will never be confused with a national assessment of the population who are *not* Ivy League business school graduates.)

Surveys of more diverse populations over the past several years, however, have resulted in similar outcomes: Networking is always at the top; mass mailings, always at the bottom. What they affirm is that generating one's own job leads—being an active rather than a passive job searcher—is exponentially more effective than depending on direct mail, print advertising, and recruitment specialists.

This is not to suggest that you should ignore these three less effective avenues to market. It does mean that allocating attention to them in roughly the same proportion as the potential payoff for each probably is the sensible way to go. Let's cover the three "lower yield" avenues to market first, so you can have them working for you without a disproportionate amount of time and thought.

Executive Recruiters

The two types of recruiters to be aware of—just so you know the distinction—are *retainer firms* (which receive their fees up front, whether they complete an assignment or not), and *contingency firms* (which don't get paid until a placement is made). Retainer firms are considered by many the more savory of the two, and indeed usually work on the higher level positions. Many contingency firms are just as respectable and effective, however.

To guide you in choosing firms to contact, a number of executive recruitment directories are available. The most comprehensive we've seen is *The Directory of Executive Recruiters*, which lists both retainer and contingency recruiters. If you can't find it in your local library, write Kennedy Publications, Templeton Road, Fitzwilliam, NH, 03447, or call 1-800-531-0007. Specify the "Job-Seeker Edition," which lists 2,200 search firms in the United States, Mexico, and Canada (indexed by function, industry, and geography), and includes 100 pages of text on conducting a job search. It's available for $39.95. Entries indicate whether a recruitment firm will accept unsolicited resumes, but unfortunately does not rate these companies on their effectiveness.

You should be able to narrow your list of target recruiting companies down to 20 or so, concentrating on those that handle your specialty. Include a few close enough for you to call on, as well. Sometimes (not always, or even frequently) you'll be able to start a relationship with a recruiter willing to go the extra hundred yards for you, if not the full mile. Occasionally you'll be able to get tips on the quality of your resume, the general job availability climate within your particular market segments, and the names of other companies in your area that might be hiring.

Marketing Strategy with a Recruiter

Start with a phone call, both to permit a personal introduction and to practice your marketing skills. Ask the receptionist to speak with someone in your specialty, by both industry and function. That way, you'll be covering two fronts simultaneously:

> "Hello. May I speak with the counselor who handles lab technicians in the health care field"?
> *(If there is no activity in your specialty, waste no more of your time; go on to the next firm. If you get through to the right person,*

present your case clearly and succinctly, and work for an interview just as you would with a target employer. The reason is that you want to make a positive impression on this recruiter— not just for positions he may be working with right now, but for those that may come up in the next several months. For example:)

"Hello, this is Brice Worley. I'm a lab technician at Quinnipiac Medical Center, and I'm wondering what openings you're working on in the health care field?"

(Let's say your recruiter has lab technician openings, but only in the pharmaceutical industry. If this area also appeals to you, you can rework your resume accordingly before mailing it in, or continue to try setting up a personal appointment. From there, the conversation could go in any one of several directions.)

"Why not send me a resume; then, we can talk."

(Not bad; at least you'll be sending your resume to someone you've spoken to, and be able to follow up. A good cover letter for such a situation appears on page105.)

Or,

"Hi, Brice. So what's been happening with you, lately"?

(This gives you a chance to synopsize your situation, mentioning what you are most proud of accomplishing in your last or current position. If you are "between jobs," don't hide the fact. Mention your flexibility and your willingness to redo your resume to reflect it.)

Or,

"Why not come by and talk for a few minutes."

(You got your interview. Before you go in, read Chapters 2 and 3 of Conquer Interview Objections, *for tips on interviewing with an executive recruiter.)*

Or,

"Sorry, we don't have anything in your area right now."

(Ask follow-up questions to be sure: (1) you're talking to the right person, and (2) there might be a reason to send in a resume for a possible job opportunity down the road.)

There's one other possible avenue to explore here. Some recruiters make it a practice to generate business by introducing

48 Cranapple Place
New Canaan, CT   06840
February 6, 1988

Mr. William Andrews
Steiniger Search of
   Fairfield County, Inc.
15 Forest Street
Stamford, CT   06901

Dear Bill:

Thank you for your willingness to review my resume. As I mentioned in our
phone conversation Tuesday, I am seeking a marketing position with a bank or
financial services firm. As a secondary priority, I would consider a
finance/treasury position with a middle-market company in the metropolitan
New York area.

My experience at Corning Works has provided me with unique insights into
commercial and investment banking, as well as the treasury needs of medium-
sized and multinational companies. Since 1976 I have developed excellent
relationships with business professionals in Connecticut, New Jersey and New
York due, in part, to my active affiliation with local and national cash
management associations.

Please let me know if I can provide you with any additional information. I
would be pleased to meet with you at your convenience, and will call you
next week to see when you might have 15 minutes or so to spend with me.

Sincerely,

Richard L. Sauer

Enclosure

outstanding candidates to prospective clients, to demonstrate the quality of people they represent. If your counselor works this way, elevate your candidacy to this level by informing him of your strengths—particularly as they relate to the marketplace he covers. Find out what openings the firm is working on and in what specific fields your counselor works successfully. If he believes it is worth making a few cold calls on your behalf, you'll be that much further ahead.

Call your recruiter every other week or so—not so often as to become a nuisance, but often enough to be kept in mind. After your first meeting, write your counselor and enclose another resume to be sure your situation is fresh in his mind. (An example of such a cover letter follows.)

                                   Rosemarie Myers
                                   66 West 79th Street
                                   New York, NY   10024
                                   December 27, 1987

Mr. M. Dale Schuldt
Heidrick & Struggles
12457 Black Rock Turnpike
Fairfield, CT   06430

Dear Dale:

    It was a pleasure meeting you last week. Thanks for taking the time to discuss and analyze various possibilities for my future.

    In addition to GTE Corp., U.S. Tobacco is involved in several sports marketing events as well. Other than those two, I'm not aware of any Fairfield County corporations active in sports marketing.

    At this time, however, I am still hopeful of finding a full-time position with a publication. I am close to a job offer from two different Fairchild publications, and am currently working on four different freelance pieces. I would prefer full-time employment to freelance, but can use assignments like these to supplement a full-time position later on, if I have to.

    Thanks again for your advice. I will keep you posted regarding any further developments. Meantime, please keep me in mind for situations you think might be a good match for my background.

                                   Best,

                                   Rosemarie Myers

Employment Agencies

Except for a few specialized firms (Robert Half in accounting, for example) most employment agencies work a relatively small territory, rarely transcending a metropolitan area. You can get a pretty good idea of their effectiveness by the number of ads they run in your local paper, and of their ethical standing by checking with the Better Business Bureau.

After you find out which agencies in your metropolitan area are active in your industry or function, call each of them. Be sure to speak with a counselor who specializes in your field—or at least has some experience with it. Send a resume and cover letter only after you have a personal emissary in each office who can be on the lookout for opportunities that may interest you. (As mentioned in Chapter 3, send a version of your resume without an Objective, unless there is only a specific opportunity of interest to you.)

Like executive recruiters, employment agencies subsist on the fees of their client companies. Counselors "on the lookout" for you, therefore, will be largely on the lookout for situations in their clients' interest; yours only by implication. This is not because they are by nature callous, but because they are in business, and simply don't have the time to both counsel job seekers (for which they are not paid) and make a living as well. The good ones will offer useful tips if asked direct questions. Just don't expect them to spend a substantial amount of time protecting *your* interests.

Newspaper Want Ads and Display Ads

Even though the odds are long of getting a job through classified advertising, it is worth spending at least a few minutes each day scanning the ads for jobs that would seem to be on target for you. After all, if no matches were made this way, the practice would soon stop. Accept it for what it is: a long shot, at best; worth a little, but not a lot of your time.

First of all, pick your spots carefully. There could be hundreds—even thousands, of other respondents. Your qualifications should be right on the money. One natural tendency when looking at the ads is to fantasize.

"I'll bet I could do that," won't do. After going through the qualifications one by one, you should be able to say—with complete honesty—"That sounds exactly like me." If six qualifications are listed, you should own at least five of them, without a stretch. If you still see yourself in the running, three tasks remain:

1.   Rework your resume Objective, Summary, and Experience sections to reflect those aspects of your background that match the job's specifications—precisely reflecting the sequence in which the job's qualifications are listed. (For an example, see Chapter 5.)

2.   Thoroughly research the company to ascertain the reasons for the opening and additional information about the company, which will enable you to write a cover letter more specifically positioning you as an ideal candidate for the opening. (For an example, see Chapter 5.)

3.   Wait at least a week before sending off your ad response. Early responses tend to get lost in the avalanche. Later responses are read more thoroughly because there are fewer of them.

For job ads that are good (but not great) for you—for example, you satisfy only four of the six qualifications listed, but do so very well—modify a resume and cover letter you used for a similar situation.

One other possibility afforded you by classified advertising is that corollary positions may be created when the advertised job is filled. Get in the habit of reading between the lines, particularly in the Business section display ads, to uncover possible jobs that won't be advertised for several weeks—perhaps months.

Because such ads are usually not classified by industry or function (health care and education openings are often listed in separate sections), you'll have to go through the entire section to spot likely target companies. Conduct thorough research on the company before sending in a proposal letter.

Blind ads.   Many ads not identifying the employer are placed by executive recruiters with an assignment to locate the best candidate for the position described. Your chances of getting an interview rest entirely on whether your qualifications justify further consideration.

Other blind ads are placed by employers dissatisfied with key employees, but unwilling to let them go without viable replacements. They don't want the word to get out that there is trouble in the position, for fear of destroying morale in the company and tipping off the competition.

A third source of blind ads is recruiters of less than honorable intent—without specific assignments, but looking to fatten lean candidate files with individuals whose level or function is in current general demand. In this case you won't even know if a job exists.

For all of these reasons, blind ads are even more risky than signed ads, worth answering only if your background is a virtual mirror image of the requirements sought, and only then if you can use an existing resume, adding a cover letter that matches your background to the ad in the exact sequence it was written. For an example, see page 110.

Direct Mail

The broadcast letter, a job-search variation of the shotgun approach, is the primary application of direct mail.

Because such a large volume of resumes must be generated to make a mass mailing even minimally effective, there is no way to personalize your approach. This, in essence, reduces your candidacy to that of the lowest common denominator—hardly likely to make you stand out from the thousands of others using the same approach.

NETWORKING STRATEGIES

The most effective conventional job-search marketing strategy is networking—now standard practice, even a buzzword, among job seekers and job search counselors. Reduced to bare bones, the idea is that your chances of finding a job improve in direct proportion to the number of influential people you meet in companies that have— or may have—openings. Often this is a two or three-step process, but it works.

Just think why it is that networking improves your chances to so much greater an extent than other methods:

- No fees to recruiters or employment agencies to cloud the decision-making process
- No jockeying with hundreds or thousands of competing job seekers who answer the same ads or send out similar formula mass mailings. It's just you and your prospective employer, one on one, no strings attached.

An overwhelming majority of jobs don't get advertised, any-

March 9, 1994

Box F   7667   Times 10108
The Los Angeles Times
229 West Sprinkle Street
Los Angeles, California   96501

Ladies/Gentleman:

I believe I have the ideal background for the "Vice-President, marketing and Sales" position advertised in the March 4 Los Angeles Sunday Times.

For the past five years I have directed the New York operations of Bonds Jewelers, Inc., a London and Geneva-based company producing and selling a quality line of gold and gem necklaces, rings, bracelets, earrings, pins and brooches. As Executive Vice-President, my responsibilities during this period have included the planning and execution of all of Bond's marketing strategies and advertising campaigns.

In 1990 I supervised the start-up of our Dallas retail outlet, including budgeting, financial forecasting, funding and marketing strategy. In preparing for the Dallas opening I created a comprehensive marketing plan to identify market factors unique to the Dallas area and developed a profile of the typical Dallas customer to precisely target jewelry design and selection--and subsequent publicity and advertising.

I am a goal-oriented self-starter, have a strong creative background, and am able to identify and maximize the talent of subordinates. I look forward to talking further with you about the advertised position, and am enclosing a resume for your information.

Sincerely,

Greta Hunt

Enclosure

way. (There is no need to advertise, after all, if qualified candidates for a position can be found and are willing to interview for it.) This body of available positions is often called "the hidden job market." Many of the jobs are filled quickly by those tapped into the networks mentioned in this chapter. They are "hidden" only to job seekers who don't do their homework. The trick is for you to become one of those candidates.

Setting Up Your Networks

In our networking workshops, we encourage people to seek out as many kinds of source groups as they can to broaden the base. Generating raw leads is the first step.

If this is a new kind of activity for you, start close to home and fan outward. In each category, develop 15 or more leads to be subsequently classified and qualified. Use a single sheet of paper for each category. Your long-range interests will be served only if you identify and contact at least 15 individuals in every category. Here is a core list of contact sources; perhaps you can think of others:

1. Husband or wife
2. Relatives
3. Neighbors and community contacts
4. Others who are looking for jobs
5. Professional and trade
6. Customers and clients
7. Service people (vendors and suppliers)
8. Former colleagues at previous employers
9. Graduate school, college, or high school associates
10. Acquaintances through avocations or interests
11. Acquaintances through religious affiliations

For best results, keep your network interview focused by your targeted market segments. For example, try to learn the names of two additional source people. Most important to your efforts, of course, will be key executives in one or more of your target companies—or their competitors.

Avoid asking for a job in your network interviews. Such a question may cause your interviewer enough discomfort to terminate your meeting much before you would like. If a job exists for which you may be qualified, your contact will ask you the questions that will determine how serious a candidate you might be.

In network categories 1 through 3 you'll need to be particularly specific. Uncle Marvin may not have all that accurate an idea of what you do, after all, and may need a more extensive briefing than will the former co-worker down the hall laid off in the same downsizing that hit you. By being both patient and explicit, leads may come to you from sources you would never have thought to contact. Just as importantly, you will be able to improve the quality of your lists, and more frequently include on them people both able and willing to help.

Keeping Networking Records

To keep your information organized, start with a Network Directory you can keep current and color code by level of potential. This will allow you to track all your sources and upgrade your folder to that of a "target company," if or when warranted. Include the following information:

NAME _____

COMPANY _____

TITLE _____ PHONE _____

ADDRESS _____

SOURCE _____ PHONE _____

PURPOSE OF CALL_____

_____

RESULTS _____

_____

FOLLOWUP_____

_____

_____

ADDITIONAL CONTACTS _____

_____

Accomplishing Network Objectives

You have at least three objectives in setting up and conducting any network interview:

1. To broaden the information base about your target company, or about competitors that may become target companies.

2. To make an ally of your source, to assure a continuing information base.

3. To get the names of additional source people.

Overcoming Network Call Objections

We say setting up *and* conducting the network interview, because there may be instances where your source may not agree to see you. If you are persistent (but not a pest), however, you may still extract enough information to make the call worthwhile.

This takes lots of practice. Early on, your tendency will be to say "Thanks anyway" if you get turned down for a meeting, and end it there. As your technique improves, however, you'll learn to use your time more productively—whether in a face-to-face interview or on the phone.

In trying to reach your contact for the first time you may run into resistance from her secretary. Most are trained to be excellent gatekeepers and are inclined to give cold callers a hard time. Be polite but persistent, and if all else fails, offer to write your contact first if you think pursuing this lead is worth your time.

Specific Networking Questions

In both your phone and personal network interviews, frame your questions with the degree of specificity that will help you most. If you already have the name of someone to whom you would report if there happened to be an opening, for example, you'd ask:

> "Do you know anything about Randy Warhole, who runs the purchasing department at Tijuana Lox?"

This would indicate that all you need before making a specific proposal to Tijuana Lox, one of your prime target companies, is a little more information about your prospective boss so you can do a better job of writing your cover letter. There are many levels of information useful to you, all the way down to *identifying* a prospective boss, or testing the validity of a rumor that a new product line *in your specialty* would create new jobs in your target company. Identify a company you'd like to work for, then find one or more inside contacts to provide you with information. To help you determine whether an opening exists or might soon exist, ask questions that will help you extract as much information of value to you as you can, and any others relevant to your situation:

- What are the possibilities of a merger or acquisition?
- Is expansion likely—the addition of one or more product or service lines?
- Are sales up (and likely to stay there)?
- Are any new activities scheduled that may require someone with your capabilities?
- Is the company experiencing any particular problems (that a person with your background could help solve?)

Because of where you've worked or what you've accomplished, the interviewer may want to pick your brain and have neither information *nor* a possible position to talk about. This is a calculated risk you must take, of course, so just be aware that some network or information interviews may be a waste of your time. Even so, such situations can sometimes be turned to your advantage.

The name of this game is "marketplace." Let's assume that you have some information of value to your interviewer about your ex-company or any of its competitors, or about people at one or more of these companies. After answering a few of the interviewer's questions (within the bounds of industry ethics, of course), get in a few of your own. This may mean changing the subject, but it is essential that you address *your* agenda relatively early in the conversation, before you have traded away any information advantage. Here are a few kinds of breakthrough questions that can open up your agenda:

"What's happening over at Software Delite with that new Unix program they said was such a breakthrough?"

"Who do you know who's looking for a good (*your position or function*)?"

"I've heard there's some activity at (*interviewer's previous em-*

ployer; or a company whose top management is known well to the interviewer). Is it okay if I use your name in trying to set up something there?'

"*(Name of subsidiary of interviewer's company or other company known well by interviewer)* interests me considerably. Who should I talk with there to introduce myself? Is there any way you can grease the skids for me?"

Seldom will your leads be so fully formed that you can reel off a job description, and then set up an interview with the "right person" in a company you have targeted. Sometimes your contact—for any number of reasons—will not want her name associated with your inquiry. In a situation like this, you're on your own. On page 117 is a letter written under such constraints that may be helpful to you in a similar situation.

With every information interview, your portfolio of target companies will change. Intelligence of various kinds will cause you to drop some companies, add others, and escalate your level of interest in still others. Following is a form to help you keep track of companies on your "A" list. Keep it with the other company information to inform job interviews as they develop:

COMPANY _____

ADDRESS _____

CITY & STATE _____ ZIP _____

CONTACT PERSON _____

TITLE _____ PHONE _____

POSSIBLE ADDITIONAL CONTACTS _____

_____

LINES OF BUSINESS _____

ANNUAL REVENUES _____# OF EMPLOYEES _____

BASIC APPEAL OF COMPANY _____

_____

PROBLEMS I CAN SOLVE AT COMPANY _____

_____

_____

INFORMATION YET NEEDED _____

_____

_____

_____

Immediately after each networking or information interview (or call), add new data to your target company's folder, to help you determine the next steps.

GENERAL INTEREST AND INDUSTRY-SPECIFIC LIBRARY SOURCES

General Interest Directories

Business Organizations, Agencies, and Publications Directory
Business Periodicals Index (350 industries and functions listed)
Corporate 1000
Directory of Corporate Affiliations (U.S. Public Companies; U.S. Private Companies; International Public and Private Companies)
Directory of Directories
Dun's Business Identification (fiche)
Dun's Employment Opportunities Directory
Dun's Million Dollar Directory (Volumes I, II, and III)
Dun's Regional Business Directory
Encyclopedia of Associations
Encyclopedia of Business Information Sources
International Corporate 1000
Macmillan Directory of Leading Private Companies
Small Business Sourcebook
Standard & Poor (Industry Surveys; Corporation Listings; Directory of Company Officers)
Standard Directory of Advertisers
Thomas Register
World Business Directory

RICHARD R. FARSON * 212 37th Street * **Lindenhurst, NY 11757**

September 15, 1994

Mr. James Coulos
Vice President, Public Affairs
Accidental Oil Corporation
18 West 34th Street
New York, NY   10017

Dear Mr. Coulos:

My sources indicate that for the past several months Accidental has been looking into the feasibility of establishing an audio lab, partially for purposes of improving executive security both domestically and abroad. You may even have such an installation underway right now.

In any case, my specialty for the last ten years has been in the area of audio analysis, voice identification and tape enhancement. I designed and currently supervise the Forensic Audio Laboratory of the New York City Police Department's Communications Division. I am also responsible for the 911 Tape Logging System, which as you probably know is the largest such operation in the world.

There are innumerable applications for the kind of experience I have had since 1981 and I welcome the opportunity to see how they might match Accidental's current or anticipated needs.   Within the next few days I will call to see when your schedule permits us to discuss this matter further.   If it turns out that this particular area is not your responsibility, I will appreciate your referral to the appropriate person.

Sincerely,

Richard R. Farson

Enc.:   Resume

RRF/dl

Industry-specific Directories

American Architects' Directory
American Hospital Association Guide to the Health Care Field
American Library Directory
Automotive News Market Data Book
Chemical Engineering Catalog
Commercial Real Estate Broker's Directory
Conservation Yearbook
Corporate Finance Bluebook
Design News
Directory of the Computer Industry
Directory of Management Consultants
Dun & Bradstreet Reference Book of Transportation
Dun's Industrial Guide: The Metalworking Directory
Editor and Publisher Market Guide
Electrical/Electronic Directory
Electronic Design's Gold Book
Fairchild's Textile and Apparel Financial Directory
International Petroleum Register
Kline Guide to the Paper & Pulp Industry
Literary Market Place: The Directory of American Book Publishing
Magazine Industry Market Place
Moody's Manuals (for various industries)
O'Dwyer's Directory of Corporate Communications
O'Dwyer's Directory of Public Relations Agencies
Polk's World Bank Directory
Printing Trades Blue Book
Progressive Grocer's Marketing Guidebook
Standard & Poor's Security Dealers of North America
Standard Directory of Advertising Agencies
Telephony's Directory of the Telephone Industry
The Uncle Sam Connection, a Guide to Federal Employment
Thomas Register of American Manufacturers
Whole World Oil Directory
Who's Who in Advertising
Who's Who in Composition and Typesetting
Who's Who in Electronics
Who's Who in Insurance
Who's Who in Water Supply and Pollution Control
World Airline Record

On Computer

Infotrac (journal and newspaper index)

Business Dateline OnDisc (business articles in local, state, and regional journals and newspapers)

ProQuest (business articles in newspapers and magazines)

Standard & Poor's Corporations (public and private companies and biographical listings)

Ultimate Job Finder (4,500 sources of trade and specialty journals)

ADDITIONAL READING

Bolles, Richard N. *What Color Is Your Parachute?* Berkeley, CA: Ten Speed Press, 1971. Popularized the concept of networking as a basic job-search technique when this book first appeared 20 years ago.

Dalyrmple, Douglas J. *Marketing Management: Strategy and Cases.* New York: John Wiley & Sons, 1986. Solid presentation of basic marketing definitions and techniques. Chapter 5 features segmentation and positioning.

Levinson, Jay Conrad. *Guerrilla Marketing: Secrets for Making Big Profits From Your Small Business.* Boston: Houghton Mifflin Company, 1984. Written for the entrepreneur, but equally useful for the average job hunter.

Lucht, John. *Rites of Passage at $100,000: The Insider's Guide to Practically Everything About Executive Job Changing.* New York: The Viceroy Press, distributed by Henry Holt & Company, Inc., 1993. Good information—other than an over-dependence on direct mail as a marketing tactic. See especially Appendix I, "Behind the Scenes with the retainer recruiter."

Welch, Mary Scott. *Networking: The Great New Way for Women to Get Ahead.* New York: Harcourt Brace Jovanovich, 1980) Not as "new" as it was in 1980, but still contains good information on finding, starting, and using networks.

5

Overcoming Resume Objections

The flexible resume will help you overcome a good number of the objections a would-be employer might have to your candidacy. Because your resume is targeted to a specific opportunity rather than written to present you as the best candidate for every job you might ever consider, many of the reasons for *not* considering you will by definition disappear.

If readers of your resume or cover letter take exception to the way you have presented yourself in *any* version you write, however, it will be for one of two reasons:

1. You have violated one or more of the principles of clarity, content, or appearance described in Chapter 3; or

2. You have not satisfactorily presented yourself to either offset or take advantage of your particular situation (covered in Chapter 5 of *Conquer Interview Objections*).

On the following pages are a number of before-and-after resumes that we hope will help impede any tendency you might have for making the same mistakes—for the first reason mentioned above. As our examples we'll use resumes that represent several different occupations and levels, so that you can adapt any ways of wording or positioning you think might improve your presentation.

CONTENT, CLARITY, AND APPEARANCE PROBLEMS

In Chapter 3 we reported the results of a poll taken among line managers and human resource executives to find out what was most important to them in deciding whether to initiate further contact with a prospective employee introduced to them by resume. Actually, they went further. Many said they would not even *read* a resume that violated one or more of the characteristics they considered crucial, let alone consider its owner as a viable candidate.

A Resume Reader's Hit List

The reasons for rejection our survey respondents gave for those resumes they felt deserved it appear below in the form of a "hit list" divided into three categories of Content, Clarity, and Appearance. A miscue of omission or commission in any one of the 23 areas, they judged, could be enough to knock a candidate out of the running. Instead of using a single resume for each of the lapses, we've conserved paper by choosing resumes that include at least two of those errors listed below.

Content

[ ] Excessive space devoted to items not directly related to career (detailed personal data, lengthy descriptions of jobs related to former careers).

[ ] Employment gaps not sufficiently played down or explained.

[ ] Sequence of major headings inappropriate to level.

[ ] Career-related volunteer experience not effectively treated or developed.

[ ] Accomplishments insufficiently treated, or not quantitatively stated, where appropriate.

[ ] Inappropriate or attention-getting wording or phrasing.

[ ] Objective, Summary, or Experience entries over or underwritten, or otherwise badly written.

Clarity

[ ] Descriptions of jobs or accomplishments longer than four lines, causing difficult reading.

[ ] Job objective or experience summary missing or not clearly stated.

[ ] Grammatical, syntactical, or spelling errors or inconsistencies.

[ ] Personal data (name, address, phone numbers) not immediately identifiable.

[ ] Job history not stated in reverse chronological order.

[ ] Use of functional resume obscures job-related strengths.

[ ] Entries or dates arranged in confusing fashion.

Appearance

[ ] Tacky typing or reproduction job.

[ ] Poor paper quality.

[ ] Vibrant, bizarre, or offbeat paper color or style.

[ ] Typographical errors.

[ ] Gratuitous, attention-getting visual effects (wild or mixed type styles, brochure format, photographs).

[ ] Paper size other than 8 1/2" x 11".

[ ] Length of more than two pages (with certain exceptions).

[ ] Inappropriate format for level.

[ ] Margins too narrow, insufficient vertical spacing, or inadequate variation in type face or font.

Some items on the list lend themselves more to examples than others. "Offbeat paper color" and "poor paper quality," for example, are difficult to show in a book printed on white paper of uniform quality. (We defined these boundaries of taste in Chapter 4.) Showing "photographs" would be unnecessarily cruel and incriminating (not to mention possibly litigious), and "Typographical errors," eminently worth searching for and eliminating on one's own resume, seem less than worthy of inclusion on a sample resume for that reason alone. All of this is by way of explaining why not every item on the list is represented in the following "before and after" examples.

Following the before-after section is a selection of resumes prepared for specific target positions. The accompanying paragraphs will help you understand each individual's situation, and why the action taken was appropriate. In both sections, all names, addresses, and backgrounds have been changed.

BEFORE-AND-AFTER RESUME EXAMPLES

Health Care Executive

Mary Linley has a lot to offer as a leader in the health care field, and has articulated her background well, for the most part. Here is where she fell short, however:

1. Her objective for this version of her resume—top job in a start-up situation—should have been buttressed by a Summary or Profile emphasizing qualifications and accomplishments matching the job's requirements.

2. The various elements of each of Mary's previous jobs need more crisp delineation, which could have been attained with creative use of spacing and type.

3. Her achievements in each job are buried in single, long paragraphs of as many as 12 lines each. This causes difficulty for the reader, both in wading through the solid type and in identifying those specific aspects of her background that may be most relevant to the open position.

Following Mary's original resume on pages 125–126 is a reworked version of her page one to show how the suggestions above could have been incorporated.

Purchasing Director

Henry Travers has an excellent background, but has been given some bad advice regarding the preparation of his resume:

1. It is an all-purpose, rather than flexible, resume and lacks an objective for the specific position he is seeking. (This is not to recommend preparing separate resumes in response to every open position, but at least one for every *kind* of position sought.)

2. Similarly, although the Summary Mr. Travers has written may be right on target for one or more openings that come his way, he needs to rewrite it as often as he responds to openings for which specific job requirements are known, *in a sequence that matches the prioritized needs of the hiring company.*

3. Finally, someone apparently told Mr. Travers that resumes longer than one page were the kiss of death. For a person of his experience (10 years or longer, that is), there is usually no such stigma. What *is* hurting Mr. Travers is that his powerful record is virtually lost in the resume's small type size and narrow margins. An argument could be made for combining some of the Experience entries to cut down on number of words used, but the primary fault is with appearance and clarity rather than content.

Following Mr. Travers' original resume on page 129 is the first page of a version somewhat easier to read, with another Summary

MARY LINLEY, Ph.D.
4808 Cantremember Lane
Vancouver, WA   99473
(H) 206-555-8995
(W) 206-555-1511

OBJECTIVE

To create a premier mental health organization committed to the delivery of quality services, staff development and understanding of customer needs.

PROFESSIONAL EXPERIENCE

Director
Synectics,
1986-Present

Founder of Synectics, Inc. Synectics, Inc. is a consulting practice specializing in organizational assessment and development, strategic problem-solving, team building, executive coaching and training initiatives which establish a leadership culture, applied leadership skills and increase staff participation. The firm's clients have included Fortune 500 corporations, major non-profit organizations and a number of community-based mental health and social service agencies. The focus of Synectics, Inc.'s consulting services is to improve the quality of services offered by an organization though the strategic development and empowerment of the workforce at all organizational levels to achieve organizational objectives.

Clinical Director
Cabot Group
Home Program
1983-86

Responsible for the administration and leadership of a community-based residential treatment program servicing severely disturbed inner-city children and adolescents. Supervised six multidisciplinary treatment teams in the delivery of clinical inpatient and outpatient services, community outreach and support services to families with children in placement. Developed and utilized an innovative multi-disciplinary team approach to the provision of treatment services and case management. Implemented standards for program licensure, accreditation and JCHA approval for emergency transitional crisis beds in partnership with Seattle Children's Psychiatric Center.

Director,
Telecollege
Therapy Ctr
Ball State
College
1982-83

Developed and administered a special service program providing clinical services and higher education courses to disabled students. Provided clinical and counseling services to students and faculty.

Assoc. Director
Bonnie Brae
Treatment Center
1979 - 1982

Responsible for the management, staff training, program development and clinical services for three treatment units servicing emotionally disturbed clients including a transitional intensive care unit.

Psychologist
Counseling Center
State University

Responsible for individual counseling, vocational counseling, testing and case management Montana consultation.

Consultant
School
1977 - 1979

Responsible for clinical services, staff Maplebrook consultation and diagnostic assessment.

EDUCATION

Ph.D
1982

Clinical Psychology
Montana State University
Missoula, Montana

B.A.
1974

Psychology
Olympic College
Bremerton, WA

AFFILIATIONS

Connecticut Psychological Association
The Organizational Development Network
The Human Resource PLanning Society

PROFESSIONAL LICENSURE

Washington #1141
Montana #7189

PUBLICATIONS

"Inferences of mental illness from noninvolvement." Journal of Personality.
1985.

MARY L. LINLEY, Ph.D.

4808 Cantremember Lane, Vancouver, WA   98473
Work: (206) 645-8995   Home: (206) 645-1511

OBJECTIVE

To create a premier mental health organization committed to the delivery of quality services, staff development, and understanding of customer needs.

SUMMARY

Clinical psychologist with 17 years experience in variety of mental health settings. Strong administrator with eight years experience heading successful corporate consulting practice. Extensive background in counseling and diagnostic assessment for client universe including adults, adolescents, and children. Innovative leader with outstanding program development record.

PROFESSIONAL EXPERIENCE

**Director,
Synectics, Inc.**

Founded consulting practice specializing in organizational assessment and development, strategic problem-solving, team building, executive coaching and training initiatives.

1986 - Present

* Teach corporate and institutional clients to achieve organizational objectives through quality strategic development and empowerment of workforce at all levels

* Establish a leadership culture by encouraging applied leadership skills and increased staff participation

* Market program to such repeat clients as Fortune 500 corporations, major non-profit organizations, and community-based mental health and social service agencies

* Increased client base by at least 30% every year since inception; consistently meet all revenue and profit goals

**Clinical Director,
Astor Group Home
Program
1983 - 1986**

Directed community-based residential treatment center servicing severely disturbed inner-city children and adolescents, delivering both inpatient and outpatient services

* Supervised six multidisciplinary treatment teams in delivery of community outreach and support services to families with children in placement

* Developed and utilized innovative multidisciplinary team approach to provision of treatment services and case management

**Director, Clearwater
Center for Counseling
1982 - 1983**

Developed and administered special service program providing clinical services and higher education courses to disabled students. Supplied clinical and counseling services to 185 students and faculty members.

written to match as closely as possible the following position. Although we've simulated a newspaper ad to transmit the job's requirements, Mr. Travers could have come by this information from a variety of other sources.

PURCHASING
Graphics Purchasing Supervisor

Resp for interfacing with both publishing divisions & outside vendors to guide promotional purchases. Implements the purchasing of catalogs, promotional materials, point-of-purchase displays & direct mail components. Extensive exp in graphics purchasing and/or mfg bkgd in graphics including knowledge of 4-color process required. Computer exp a plus. Resumes stating salary requirements to: Personnel Dept.

> Reed & Replica, Publishers
> 4200 Grand Isle Blvd
> Detroit, MI 48310
> An Equal Opportunity Employer

Computer Coordinator

Delbert Kantor has not served himself well. First, he is guilty of several typographical errors. Second, page one of his functional resume covers three areas of expertise and a paragraph of accomplishments, along with his Objective and Summary. Because he gives no dates for his employment at the four companies listed on page two, one wonders if a job hopping problem is the reason he decided against a chronological resume. Even if this is not the case, most prospective employers will be suspicious of his motives.

There is another basic flaw in Delbert's resume, particularly crucial because it appears near the top of the first page: Rather than utilize valuable Summary space for a skills and accomplishments matchup with a specific position, Delbert has chosen instead to write a thumbnail autobiography—beginning with his first job and working his way forward. Most readers won't get beyond this point, particularly since he unnecessarily introduces a possible age problem by announcing his 28 years of work experience, and uses a rambling style to introduce himself.

Neither does Delbert help himself by devoting most of the space he has allocated for "Operations Experience" to an essay on the history of computer hardware and software, a gross waste of precious space.

Following this resume on page 131 is a version of a page one that works more effectively.

HENRY TRAVERS   Cornelia Place, Ipsheming, Michigan   616/934-6114

Summary: A manager and administrator of Purchasing with corporate/manufacturing and full service management experience. Major Strengths in team building, planning and project directing. Additional skills in the areas of negotiating, budgeting/cost control, design/development, and distribution. A dependable, thorough, and well organized planner who is innovative and communicates effectively.

Experience:

Information Service
Manager
Central Area
Publishing Unit
1992-1993
(Publishing/Advertising
service organization)
Lansing, MI

- Responsible for the administration and technical management of the processing, typesetting, printing and distribution of over 2000 reports and all promotional materials.
- Oversaw the maintenance of all information pertinent to membership Publishing unit files and print orders.
- Directed all mailroom, stockroom activities and facilities maintenance.
- Established an internal control system for tracking all circulation reports.
- Upgraded all telecommunications and all office service maintenance activities to include; fax equipment, copier equipment, PC's, typewriters, and dictating equipment.
- Responsible for the preparation of the annual department budget of $3+ million and the approval for payment of expense charged to the department.
- Employed, discharged, supervised, trained, reviewed performance and recommended compensation of personnel assigned to this department of 22.

Central Purchasing
Manager
Ernst & Young
1977-1990
("Big 6" CPA firm)
Detroit, MI

- Managed a $10+ million annual budget allocated to overall production of print media, including national/international mailings and distributions.
- Achieved $3 million in savings over the last five years, through efficient purchasing methods and management controls.
- Integrated activities of, and met with, graphics, editorial, production personnel, and vendors to assure that quality control standards/deadlines were met and that costs stayed within budget.
- Purchased and coordinated installation of new logo signage for 130+ U.S. offices.
- Coordinated the creation of a world-wide Graphic Identify Systems manual.
- Established and maintained purchase agreements/national contracts for capital equipment, technical and educational materials, graphic arts, and office supplies.
- Initiated a national/international premium program.
- Worked closely with the office of the chairman and department heads to establish annual budgets.
- Negotiated agreements with major car leasing companies and hotel chains, to establish volume discounts.
- Supervised, annually, relocations of 400+ national/international executives.

Senior Buyer -
Standard Brands
Products, 1973-1977
(Manufacturer of
roller blades)
New York, NY

- Directed production of promotional materials with an annual budget of $3+ million.
- Managed purchasing of all office supplies, including plating of manufactured product parts.
- Qualified vendors routinely for high-quality, cost-effective foil labels, decals, inserts, four-color silk screen displays (vinyl and fiberboard), polyethylene/kraft bags, display cards and plastic bags.
- Procure printed folding boxes, corrugated boxes, and POP displays.

Printing & Production
Manager - Chicago
Chamber of Commerce
1972-1973
Chicago, IL

- Managed in-house typesetters and freelance graphic art designers producing newsletters, posters, invitations, programs, and books.
- Participated actively in fundraising activities (e.g., the "Navy Pier" and "Business and Labor Navy Pier").
- Implemented direct mail programs (volume in the millions).
- Responsible for a $2+ million budget.

Assistant Purchasing
Manager - Consumers
Club, 1963-1972
(Credit cards)
New York, NY

- Established inventory controls to monitor office equipment, furniture, and fixtures.
- Assisted Purchasing Director in buying promotional printing.
- Worked closely with marketing/advertising departments to develop POP displays/ads and special programs.

Education: B.B.A., Advertising, Hunter College (CUNY).

Affiliation: National Association of Purchasing Management of Michigan and Illinois.

Awards: AGI - American Graphics Institute; PIA - Printing Industries of America; PIMNY - Printing Industries Metropolitan Detroit.

HENRY TRAVERS   **Cornelia Place, Ipsheming, Michigan**   **616/934-6114**

SUMMARY: Graphics purchasing director with strong background in publishing and printing services. Extensive experience directing purchase and production of four-color catalogs, promotional materials, and point-of-purchase displays for national and international mailings and distributions. Proficient with Quark Xpress.

EXPERIENCE:

Information Services Manager
Central Area
Publishing Unit
1992-1993
(Publishing/Ad service)
Lansing, MI

- Responsible for the administration and technical management of the processing, typesetting, printing and distribution of over 2000 reports and all promotional materials.

- Oversaw the maintenance of all information pertinent to membership files and print orders.

- Directed all mailroom, stockroom activities and facilities maintenance.

- Established an internal control system for tracking all circulation reports.

- Upgraded all telecommunications and all office service maintenance activities to include: fax and copier equipment, PC's, typewriters, and dictating equipment.

- Responsible for the preparation of the annual department budget of $3 + million and the approval for payment of expenses charged to the department.

- Employed, discharged, supervised, trained, reviewed performance and recommended compensation of personnel assigned to this department of 22.

Central Purchasing Manager
Ernst & Young
1977-1992
("Big 6" CPA firm)
Detroit, MI

- Managed a $10 + million annual budget allocated to overall production of print media, including national/international mailings and distributions.

- Saved $3 million over the last five years through efficient purchasing methods and management controls.

- Integrated activities of, and met with, graphics, editorial, production personnel, and vendors to assure that quality control standards/deadlines were met and that costs stayed within budget.

- Purchased and coordinated installation of new logo signage for 130 + U.S. offices.

- Coordinated the creation of a world-wide Graphic Identity Systems manual.

- Established and maintained purchase agreements/national contracts for capital equipment, technical and educational materials, graphic arts, and office supplies.

130

Delbert Kantor
227 Jefferson Street
Genera, IL 60134
(312) 232-1066

Objective:
Challenging employment in middle (computer) management and/or liaison between data processing and other departments.

Summary of Experience:
In my twenty eight years in the work place I have a variety of expert skills. Starting as an accounting clerk, being promoted to Junior accountant. I enhanced my career by studying computer science (on the job), by taking an entry level computer job and working my way up to Senior Operator, Operations Manager, Data Processing Manager, MIS Director and finally Computer Coordinator. My duties ranged from supervising a department of ten people to budgeting for capitol expenditures (computer systems for the entire corporation) overseeing the taking of inventory and everyday purchases (computer).

Experience:

Management:
Twenty one years managing has helped me fine tune my skills down to a science. I have managed accounts payable clerks, verifying clerks, data entry clerks, computer operators, computer programmers, payroll clerks, cost clerks, accounts receivable and collection personnel.

Operations:
Nineteen years in the computer area has seen many changes, not only in hardware but also in software. My first main frame was an NCR Century 100 with a software package written by in-house programs. Eighteen years later main frames are seventy-five per cent smaller but thousands of times faster and with many millions of bytes or memory (IBM AS/400) and program packages such as MAPICS (a manufacturing package, leased by IBM).

Budgetary:
Budgets consisted of salary increases, bonuses, office supplies, computer supplies (ribbons, magnetic tape, paper and forms) and capital expenditures (printers, disk drives, tape drives, memory, main frames) and UPS (uninterrupted power supplies) system.

Accomplishments:
Implemented a computer disaster recovery plan which cost the company no out of pocket expense. If recovery had to take place the bottom line to continue processing would have been time and expense. Also, implemented changes in duties, hours (computer operator) and equipment over many years with Felton which resulted in staff reduction of two data entry clerks, one programmer and one computer operator. With savings to the company of approximately seventh five thousand dollars, plus benefits. Designed new multi function forms to take the place of many old ones and saved on printing cost.

Delbert Kantor
227 Jefferson Street
Genera, IL   60134
(312) 232-1066

Equipment:
        NCR Century 100, 101, 200
        NCR Criteron 8450, 8455, 8565.
        NCR 9822 (Fault Tolerant Machine).
        NCR Tower 650
        IBM AS/400
        Macintosh SE & Plus.

Software:
        VRX & VRX/E operating system
        Unix
        In house mfg system
        Boss/3 on-line system
        Cimpro-Datalogix mfg system
        Mapics-IBM mfg system
        Macdraw, Macwrite, Macpaint, etc.

Places worked:
        N.W. Ayer Worldwide, Inc./F&C International
        599 Adams Street
        Chicago, IL   60105
        Computer Coordinator

        Hammel-Riglander & Company, Inc.
        435 Hudson Street
        New York, NY   10014
        Senior Computer Operator

        Jacoby Bender, Inc.
        62-10 Northern Blvd.
        Woodside, NY   11377
        Junior Computer Operator

        Metro-Goldwyn-Mayer, Inc.
        New York, NY and Culver City, GA.
        Junior Accountant

Education:

        Various N.C.R. and Datalogix courses.
        NYU 1978-1980 took several courses in computer science.
        Electronic Computer Programming INstitute graduated May 1972, Programming
            course
        Baruch College attended between 1968-70 took several courses in
            accounting.
        Midwood High School-graduated 1963, Accounting major.

DELBERT KANTOR
227 Jefferson Street
Genera, IL   60134
(312) 232-1066

OBJECTIVE: MIS Director or Computer Coordinator

SUMMARY: Extensive supervisory background in information services and
                correlated areas. Accomplished problem-solver and trouble shooter.
                Budgetary authority includes capital expenditure at corporate level.

Equipment: Software:
NCR Century 100, 101, 200   VRX & VRX/E Operating System
NCR Criterion 8450, 8455, 8555, 8565   Unix
NCR 9822 (Fault Tolerant Machine)   In-house mfg system
NCR Tower 650   Boss/3 on-line system
IBM AS/400   Mapics-IBM mfg system
Macintosh SE & Plus   Macdraw,Macwrite,Macpaint

EXPERIENCE: N.W. AYER WORLDWIDE, Chicago, IL
                Computer Coordinator: MIS Director
1983 to
Present   * Direct MIS effort for world headquarters of international
                   advertising agency

                * Hire, train, and supervise department of 10 computer operators,
                   programmers, and support personnel

                * Promoted from MIS Director in 1988

                Accomplishments:
                - Originated and implemented computer disaster recovery plan
                - Designed variety of multi-function replacement forms
                - Restructured department by consolidating responsibilities and
                   equipment at annual savings in excess of $75,000

                HAMMEL-RIGLANDER & COMPANY, INC., New York, NY
                Senior Computer Operator
1981
to   * Supervised seven computer operators running bank applications
1983   on daily cycle; approved tape and turnover log sheets

                * Supervised debugging of Unix and MAPICS systems

                * Recommended replacement and purchase of printers, disc drives,
                   tape drives, memory and UPS systems as necessary

Executive Secretary

Basic skills by themselves aren't nearly enough to make one a successful executive secretary. Problem-solving skills, as well as the ability to create an atmosphere that makes the office a smoothly functional operation, are crucial. So are such skills as flexibility and the ability to communicate well.

Karen Jordan will lose interviews to candidates applying for the same job whose skills may not equal hers, but who nevertheless have emphasized less quantifiable assets.

Also, her Experience entries could have been written in a more effective way. Following her resume on page 135 is a version showing how she could have improved her effort—and without the typographical error in her first Experience entry and the spatial error in the second.

Sales and Marketing Representative

Except for the name and the locale, Joe A. Hornblower's resume is for real. Although his high-profile approach may appeal to a few prospective employers who rate egomania as one indicator of high potential sales performance, this kind of presentation probably will repel more readers than it attracts.

The first page—except for his "customer-driven principles"—has nothing to do with job or career-related matters, and simply blows the horn for Joe. His second page (there were five in all, but we've spared you) lists his objective for a next job, and the "commitments" fulfilled in his current one. A graph compares his performance with that of the other reps in his division over a three-year period.

On the last three pages of his resume not included here, Joe correlates his performance and accomplishments with specific employers. His record is spectacular, but more than a few readers will get the feeling that his priorities are directed more toward personal gratification than they are toward company objectives. This will cost Joe a number of good opportunities, as will the typographical error on page one (page 138). Can you find it?

Bank Vice President

Marcia Shin's most grievous resume writing sin is one of carelessness. The essence of her message comes through in the "before" version, but this is a document she obviously considers of minimal

KAREN W. JORDAN
810 Sandholm Street
Aurora, CO   74630
(303) 847-9839

SKILLS: Typing 70+ WPM, Stenoscript, Lotus 123, Symphony, Chartmaster,
                 Displaywrite 3, Volkswriter, Formtools, Allways, Wang, WordPerfect

EXPERIENCE:

8/89 to   FISHER CAMARO RETAIL CORP., Boulder, Colorado
Present   Executive Secretary to Vice President, Operations/Real Estate

                 Responsible for daily, monthly and weekly reports including Sales
                 Plans, Selling Expense, Non-Profitable Stores, and Sales
                 Performance; tracking and maintaining manager salaries, manager
                 turnover and manager bonuses, updating and distributing Store
                 Address List, Division Listing, Store Opening List, Area Coordinator
                 Listing and WEekly Travel Schedules; drafting correspondence, travel
                 arrangements, special projects as assigned and general office duties

6/87 - 5/89   DATA SWITCH CORPORATION, Aspen, Colorado
                 Senior Secretary

                 Payroll, mailroom, supply room and cafeteria operations, scheduled
                 Quality Training Program for 600+ employees; coordinated employee
                 day and managers' meetings, along with general office duties

6/86 - 6/87   LEAR SIEGLER INTERNATIONAL, Denver, Colorado
                 Secretary

                 Monthly financial records, check processing preparation of
                 statistical reports and general office duties.

EDUCATION:

1982   Northwood High School, Lake Placid, New York

1986   Katharine Gibbs School, Denver, Colorado
                 Information Processing
                 Honor Roll

1988   Denver Community College, Denver, Colorado
                 General Business curriculum

INTERESTS: Figure Skating (Gold Test), Aerobics

REFERENCES: Available upon request

KAREN W. JORDAN
810 Sandholm Street, Aurora, CO   74630
Work: 303/847-9839   Home: 303/414-7545

OBJECTIVE: Executive Secretary

SUMMARY: Seven years corporate administrative background. Expert at anticipating and solving complex
                problems. Effective communicator at highest levels. Katharine Gibbs honor grad. Type 70+ wpm.
                Know Stenoscript, Lotus 123, Symphony, Chartmaster, Displaywrite 3, Volkswriter, Formtools,
                Wang, etc.

EXPERIENCE: FISHER CAMARO RETAIL CORP., Boulder CO
                Executive Secretary to Vice President, Operations

1991 to
Present   * Prepare daily, monthly and weekly reports, including sales plans, selling expense and sales
                  performance

                * Update and distribute store address list, division listing, and weekly travel schedules,
                  among others

                * Draft correspondence, make travel arrangements, complete special projects as assigned

                DATA SWITCH CORPORATION, Colorado Springs, CO
                Senior Secretary
1989
to   * Supervised payroll, mailroom, supply room and cafeteria
1991
                * Scheduled Quality Training Program for 600+ employees

                * Coordinated employee day and managers' meetings

                LEAR SIEGLER INTERNATIONAL, Denver, CO
                Secretary
1988
to   * Performed general office duties, including monthly financial 1989 records, statistical reports,
1989   check processing

EDUCATION: DENVER COMMUNITY COLLEGE, Denver, CO
                1990 - General Business Curriculum

                KATHARINE GIBBS SCHOOL, Denver, CO
                1988 - Information Processing; Honor Roll

INTERESTS: Figure skating (Gold Test); Aerobics

JOE A. HORNBLOWER
Mission Statement
Absolute Performance

I constitute myself the future of the enterprise.
My accomplishments are more than the sum of my talents, education,
goals and results. My accomplishments are sourced from my
committed action and effective speaking which puts
my intentions powerfully into the world.

I declare myself as altering the course of events,
to bring into existence the possibilities
driven by my creativity.
I establish and maintain relationships
by being with the customer in such a way
that the natural outcome is our to desire to conduct
mutually beneficial business.

I have a vision and an unreasonableness
that finds authentic self-expression in bringing forth
that which is not yet.
I have the courage to initiate a conversation for action-and,
in speaking and in action,-to inspire and to free
the best in those around me.

I am 100% Customer-driven.

My principles in regard to this are:

* *Respect for the dignity and worth*
of the individual

* *Provide the finest service*
of any company in any industry

* *Demonstrate excellence in*
execution

1408 Anderson Boulevard

Unit 161

Gaithersburg, Maryland 20879 2907

Telephone: (310) 822-2200

SALES ANALYSIS BY REPRESENTATIVES

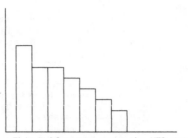

OBJECTIVE:
An association with a progressive
organization in a <u>Senior Software Sales</u>
position to the **Financial Marketplace**
which places an emphasis on:

1. Opportunity for advancement consistent
   with ability to contribute.

2. Achieving a balance between being
   product oriented and marketing driven.

3. Is dedicated and focused on customer
   issues and concerns.

This table represents the YTD revenue
productivity of each salesperson in the
local Divisional office.

As you can see, my sales contributions
equal 38% of the total sales contributions of 11 divisional Financial Sales
Specialists.

Commitments:

* To increase annual billings in **new
  financal systems** installations by no
  less than 50% each cosecutive year.

* To generate net profits from **new
  systems business** by no less than 40%
  from all major accounts on a
  quarterly basis.

* To develop new consulting engagements
  by 200% over competitors in assigned
  vertical and geographical markets.

* To create a strategic direction for
  major account penetration which would
  yield further revenue growth of $3.2
  million dollars in a three year time
  frame. In essence, provided
  leadership, not salesmanship.

Results:

1990:
  Quota: $1,000,000
  Increase: 25% over 1989
  Sales: $3,970,342
  Results: 397.03% attainment
              of annual quota

1991
  Quota:
  Increase: 20% over 1990
  Sales: $5,499,960
  Results: 458.33% attainment
              of annual quota

1992
  Quota: $1,800,000
  Increase: 50% over 1991
  Sales: $8,945,820
  Results: 496.99% attainment

JOE A. HORNBLOWER
1408 Anderson Boulevard, Gaithersburg, Maryland   20879
(301) 789-2232

OBJECTIVE: Senior Software Sales Position in the Financial Marketplace

SUMMARY: Fifteen years unparalleled success opening and developing financial
           systems sales, averaging over 400% of quota for past three years.
           Attained top 1% status in nationwide salesforce of 2600.
           "President's Club" rating for past 11 years. Accomplished trainer.

EXPERIENCE: CITRIX SYSTEMS, INC., Luthersville, MD
                <u>Senior Marketing Representative, New Business</u>
1983 to
Present   * Opened and developed accounts with Wells-Fargo Bank, Home
                    Savings, Household Bank, CitiBank, Bank of America,
                    Security Pacific, Santa Barbara Savings, etc.

                       - Maintain and enhance established relationships with 304
                         corporate officers in 38 select Fortune 500 accounts;
                         spearheaded "team selling" concept in Southeast
                         district

                       - Consult with corporate officers; conduct systems
                         analysis; define requirements; construct enterprise
                         plan and incorporate data models; deliver multimedia
                         presentations to executive committees and boards of
                         directors

                       - Write, propose and present plans and objectives; create
                         implementation and employee training schedules

                  * Produce 38% of sales among 11 divisional representatives;
                    attained top 1% status within nationwide sales force of
                    2600; achieved "President's Club" 11 consecutive years;
                    performed at 227% of quota for past six years

                  * Hired as <u>Corporate Sales Trainer</u>, with successive
                    promotions to <u>Strategic Account Manager</u>, <u>National Account
                    Manager</u> and <u>Corporate Account Manager</u>

                SUN MICROSYSTEMS, Washington, D.C.
                <u>Marketing Representative, Specialized Software</u>

1981
to   * Sold COBOL course code programming productivity software to
1983   variety of mainframe environments

                  * Immediately initiated direct sales and promotion to
                    territory, increasing volume from deficit of $290,000 to
                    $710,000 in 13 months

importance. Her use of shorthand, for one thing—including bank terms and acronyms that few outsiders would understand—will put off many readers. All entries are tersely stated. She makes no effort to document the accomplishments that led to her seven promotions in sixteen years. Her effort is so impersonal that she lists neither home address nor phone number.

The revised version on pages 142–143 tells her story in an orderly, powerful way, emphasizing the skills and accomplishments package that will raise her presentation to an interest-attracting level.

Publishing Production Director

Russell Hendrickson has an enviable professional background, but failed to communicate it to prospective employers. We substituted for his vague, unfocused Objective a Summary of career highlights and marketable skills, making it easy for a reader to put the rest of his resume in context. Missing from his final version are 15 errors of punctuation and grammar in the original that also would have caused readers to move quickly to the next candidate. Can you find them on pages 144–145?

Addendum: As a printing/publishing professional, Russell had a perfect opportunity to demonstrate his graphic and production expertise (in a tasteful, subdued fashion, of course). Instead he produced a resume with no creativity of design whatsoever, run off on the most rudimentary of dot-matrix printers.

Financial Services Market Director

Meg Thompson's biggest problem is to defend six job changes in fourteen years, several just a year or two apart. Her original resume, without either an Objective or a Summary, hurts her even more. By opening her presentation with a description of the first of these six jobs, Meg draws attention to her problem rather than to the principal strengths she could have highlighted with a strong Objective and Summary. (See pages 148–149.)

Eventually she was encouraged to do just that, adding a transitional opening entry with each job, to account for the reason for each job change. She also was counseled to deal with her perceived "job hopping" problem by bringing it up herself in the interview if the interviewer did not. Complete strategy and tactics for overcoming this and other interviewing problems can be found in Chapters 4 and 5 in *Conquer Interview Objections*. Actually, Meg forgot one

Marcia Shin
Vice President

Wells Fargo Bank
(213) 559-2864

Experience:
Specific Strengths - developed ability to negotiate and complete highly complex transactions, involving extensive legal documentation and structuring; excellent knowledge of Bank credit policies and procedures, including RAR; good administrative skills and attention to detail; excellent knowledge of Bank and its organization.

Wells Fargo Bank	1978-Present
5/89-6/91	Corporate Asset Funding
3/84-5/89	Wells Fargo Bank - Los Angeles NABC; Los Angeles Area, Eastern Division - Asset securitization for publicly rated companies for southern California middle market; helped develop marketing strategy and became leading transactor in financing of tax-beneficial limited partnerships - built own portfolio from 0 to $310MM in 3 years, with excellent AP results. Extensively utilized Bank's products, including ITS and interest rate hedges. Coached junior RMs in partnership financings.
7/83-2/84	Wells Fargo Bank - New York; Credit Analysis Unit, NABC - successfully completed credit training program.
1/83-6/83	Wells Fargo Bank - New York, NABC; Division Credit Office - participated in regionalization process transferring account responsibilities to field offices, coordinating and tracking all transfers; compiled, edited, and published a regional credit policy/procedure manual for the field offices.
1/80-12/82	Wells Fargo Bank - New York; Commercial Banking Department - credit liaison person between Head Office and corporate loan production offices around U.S.A.; coordinated all credit approvals and legal documents flowing through system. Extensive work with credit policies and procedures; attended all money allocation meetings on behalf of field offices; worked closely with RAR and federal auditors when reviewing credits and procedures; assisted in setting up RAR procedures for field offices; participated in legal process of switching offices.
1/78-1/80	Wells Fargo Bank - New York; Airlines and Aerospace Department - coordinated transfer of international airline loans from IBG to NABG; set up and supervised loan and administrative process.
4/78-11/78	Wells Fargo Bank - International, Los Angeles; Supervised Credit Department - reorganized filing system and updated credit procedures.

Previous employment:
Republic National Bank of New York - 1974 - 1977, Credit Analyst, Junior Loan Officer. Master Card - 1973/74, Credit/Collection Supervisor.

Education:
Bachelor of Arts Degree - Michigan State University
Various courses - American Institute of Banking. Various seminars - Wells Fargo N.A.

MARCIA SHIN
385 Old Colony Road, Marina del Rey, CA 90292
Office: 213/559-2864   Home: 213/472-0642

SUMMARY: Able to negotiate and complete highly complex transactions involving extensive legal documentation and structuring. Excellent knowledge of credit policies and procedures, including risk asset review. Sound administrative skills; good coach; good organizer

EXPERIENCE: WELLS FARGO BANK, Los Angeles, CA   (June 1991-Present)
             Vice President, Private Banking Group

1978 to
Present   * Handle variety of credit requests for client base with average net worth of $40MM to $50MM

             * Transact loans ranging from $5MM to $64MM, with majority falling in $10MM to $20MM range

             * Built portfolio from $75MM to $150MM in just over one year

             Corporate Asset Funding   (May 1989-June 1991)

             * Purchased assets of publicly rated companies with deal sizes from $25MM to $400MM

             Relationship Manager, N.A. Banking Group (March 1984-May 1989)

             * Helped develop marketing strategy for Southern California middle market; became leading transactor in financing of tax-beneficial limited partnerships

             * Built own portfolio from zero to $310MM in three years, with excellent account profit results

             * Extensively utilized bank products, including international trade services and interest rate hedges

             * Coached junior relationship managers in partnership financings

             Credit Analysis Unit, N.A. Banking Group   (July 1983-Feb 1984)

             * Successfully completed credit training program

             Division Credit Office   (Jan 1983 to June 1983)

             * Participated in regionalization process transferring account responsibilities to field offices, coordinating and tracking all transfers

             * Compiled, edited and published a regional credit policy and procedure manual for the field offices

142

MARCIA SHIN

Commercial Banking Department   (Jan 1980 to Dec 1982)

* Served as credit liaison between Head Office and corporate
  loan production offices throughout U.S.; coordinated all credit
  approvals and legal documents flowing through system

* Extensive work with credit policies and procedures; attended
  all money allocation meetings on behalf of field offices

Airlines and Aerospace Department   (Nov 1978 to Jan 1980)

* Coordinated transfer of international airline loans from
  International Banking Group to North American Banking Group;
  set up and supervised loan and administrative process

Wells Fargo Bank   (Los Angeles; April 1978 to Nov 1978)

* Supervised Credit Department; reorganized filing system and
  updated credit procedures

**PREVIOUS
EMPLOYMENT**:

1974-1977   REPUBLIC NATIONAL BANK OF NEW YORK
             Credit Analyst; Junior Loan Officer

1973-1974   MASTER CARD
             Credit/Collection Supervisor

RUSSELL HENDRICKSON
1420 Broadway
Van Horn, Texas   79855
(916) 555-4937

PROFESSIONAL OBJECTIVE:
Applying for Professional Career opportunity.

PROFESSIONAL EXPERIENCE:

DIRECTOR OF PRODUCTION & INVENTORY
Steck-Vaugn Company, Austin, TX
1985 - May 17, 1993

Educational publisher specializing in children, library and reference
publications. Responsible for the entire purchasing operations of books, magazine
divisions which includes audio visual, promotional, and all internal products to
insure the effective expenditures of funds to satisfy company requirements.

* Four color publisher.
* Managing staff of five.
* Assembling and controlling all budgetary production cost of new/existing
  products.
* Organize all production schedules.
* Managing all production operations from the product analysis development stage
  through the point of approval, design, editorial, typesetting, graphical
  assembly, film prep, manufacturing, and delivery of the product to the point of
  distribution.
* Controlling and forecasting all inventory functions.
* Providing technical assistance to creative (Art) department.
* Providing assistance to marketing Department.

Accomplishment: Computerization of the majority production and inventory function.

PRODUCT MANAGER
Charles E. Merrill publishing Company,Columbus, Ohio
1981 - 1983

College textbook publisher. In-charge of all the production functions of new and
existing products from the point of approval through the manufacturing and
delivery of the product to the final point of distribution.
(One through four color publisher)

PRODUCTION BUYER
Follett Publishing Company, Chicago, Illinois
1977 - 1981

Elementary and high school publisher. Responsible for the purchasing operations of
new and existing four color products as they were assigned. The functions were to
control and monitor the production schedules. (Four color publisher)

PRODUCTION BUYER AND ART DIRECTOR ASSISTANT
Benefic Press, Westchester, Illinois

1977 - 1979

Elementary textbook and audio-visual publisher. Providing assistance to my
supervisor with all the assigned responsibilities. (Four color publisher)

PRINT SHOP MANAGER
Fast Printing Company, Harvey, Illinois

1975 - 1977

Printing company specializing in four color printing. Initially hired to evaluate and recommend improvements to their production systems. Reorganized entire production operations. The result was that the company formerly under great financial strain became a money-making operation, and thus improved their financial status, reputation and credibility of the company.

EDUCATIONAL BACKGROUND:

UNIVERSITY OF ILLINOIS AT CHICAGO CIRCLE, Chicago, Illinois
Graduated 1976, B.S. Degree in Industrial Engineering.

LEWIS - ST. FRANCIS COLLEGE, Lockport, Illinois
ATtended from 1972 - 1973. Curriculum with emphasis on science and technology.

COLLEGE OF DUPAGE, Glen Ellyn, Illinois
Attended from 1978 - to 1980. Specific areas of study include:

PERSONNEL MANAGEMENT (Diploma Certificate)
   Curriculum with emphasis procedures and principles of personnel management, and the psychological approaches to personnel control.

GRAPHIC ARTS
   Curriculum with emphasis on administrative and advance print shop practices, such as typesetting, pre-preliminary operations, striping, plate making, and final assembly of operational systems.

PRODUCTION AND OFFICE MANAGEMENT
   Curriculum with emphasis on fundamental functions of modern production techniques, modern theories and practices of office management, and utilization of office space and equipment.

REFERENCES: References available upon request.

RUSSELL HENDRICKSON
1420 Broadway
Van Horn, Texas   79855
(916) 555-4937

PROFILE: Accomplished educational publishing production executive, from project inception to manufacture. Consistent on-time, on-budget record working with suppliers, freelancers and staff. Proficient in computer and disc conversion management.

EXPERIENCE: Steck-Vaughn Company, Austin, TX
<u>Director of Production & Inventory</u>

1985
to
1993
    Directed entire production and purchasing operation for book and magazine publisher of reference, library and children's publications

*   Supervised staff of five in managing all production duties from product analysis through point of approval, design, editorial, typesetting, graphic assembly, film, prep, manufacturing and delivery of product to point of distribution

*   Organized all production schedules; assembled and controlled all budgetary production costs of new and existing one-through four-color books and magazines, as well as audiovisual, promotional and internal products

*   Controlled and forecast all inventory functions; provided technical assistance to art and marketing departments

*   Supervised computerization of nearly all production and inventory functions

CHARLES E. MERRILL PUBLISHING COMPANY, Columbus, OH
<u>Production Manager</u>

1983
to
1985
    Directed all production functions for new and existing college-level product (one- through four-color), from point of approval to manufacturing and delivery of product

FOLLETT PUBLISHING COMPANY, Chicago, IL
<u>Production Buyer</u>

1979
to
1983
    Supervised purchasing operations of new and existing four-color elementary and high school product. Controlled and monitored production schedules.

BENEFIC PRESS, Westchester, IL
<u>Production Buyer and Assistant Art Director</u>

1977
to
1979
    Assisted Art Director and Production Manager to carry out all assigned duties for four-color publishing program

146

EDUCATION: UNIVERSITY OF ILLINOIS AT CHICAGO CIRCLE, Chicago, IL
1976-B.S., Industrial Engineering

LEWIS-ST. FRANCIS COLLEGE, Lockport, IL
1972-73 - Pursued science and technology curriculum

COLLEGE OF DUPAGE, Glen Ellyn, IL
1971-79 - Completed areas of study in:

Personnel Management (Diploma Certificate)
Procedures and principles of personnel management, including
psychological approaches to personnel control

Graphic Arts
Emphasis on administrative and advance print shop practices such as
typesetting, pre-preliminary operations, stripping, plate making,
and final assembly of operational systems

Production and Office Management
Emphasis on fundamental functions of modern production techniques,
modern theories and practices of office management, and utilization
of office space and equipment

Meg Thompson
234 Washington Street, Apt. 22
Brooklyn, NY 11218
(718) 138- 5522

EXPERIENCE

Information Systems, Inc.   1/ 92 to present
Manager, Data Products

Market Informations Systems data products: high-speed datafeeds and data base products to domestic and international financial service firms.

o   Define product positioning and strategy; develop business plan and financial projections for pricing analyses and sales forecasts.

o   Manage all aspects of product development and release process, including product design, testing and evaluation, product introduction and roll-out.

o   Identify market opportunities and target sales prospects for product promotion; create marketing brochures, direct mail campaigns and other sales materials;

o   Initiate sales contacts and generate leads; train sales force and sales support staff to identify sales opportunities; establish sales incentives.

Financial Systems   5/89 to 1/91
Manager, Customer Relations and Promotional Services

Developed and directed all sales promotion programs, special events and trade show exhibitions for Financial System's domestic business.

o   Exhibited services successfully at more than 115 customer sales meetings, financial conferences and industry trade shows during 1991; increased conference and show exhibits by 30% without increasing operational expenses.

o   Orchestrated annual sales conference and other special events; planned and managed program budgets; contracted with vendors; designed programs and selected speakers.

Datanet   5/87 to 5/89
Manager, Sales and Marketing

Managed all marketing and marketing communications to promote company and services to institutional market.

o   Coordinated special projects, including all phases of $1.5 million expansion of institutional sales and trading area; directed project planning, budgeting, facilities renovation, vendor contracts, system testing and user training.

o   Initiated sales campaign to increase soft dollar commitments; arranged participation in investment conferences, security analyst meetings, and trade shows; created sales promotion materials and developed monthly newsletter for institutional customers.

o   Managed press contacts; prepared all press releases and executive speeches.

General Products
Senior Financial Analyst
1/86 to 5/87

Consolidated and analyzed financial results for manufacturing division, reporting to financial controller.

o   Corporate liaison to 25 regional plant controllers to ensure accurate and timely financial reporting; designed and implemented PC-based financial package to facilitate consolidation of monthly statements.

o   Booked division's monthly, quarterly and annual earnings, taxes and depreciation to corporate accounts; analyzed results.

Business Advisors, Inc.
Consultant
8/83 to 1/86

Advised entrepreneurs on all aspects of small business start-up and new product launch.

o   Devised business entry and expansion strategies; researched market potential; reviewed operational plans and organizational design; analyzed financial projections.

o   Supported the successful launch of a mail-order catalog business.

U.S. Information Agency
Foreign Service Information Officer
8/80 to 8/83

Promoted U.S. foreign policy to journalists, government officials and advisors, and other opinion leaders.
o   Organized seminars, conferences and cultural events sponsored by the U.S. Embassy or affiliated cultural and exchange organizations.

o   Managed local media relations, initiating contact for press placement, interviews with embassy officials, or background briefings; supervised press and publications staff.

City of Minneapolis
Public Affairs Specialist
10/78 to 8/80

Publicized and promoted successful programs of city agency.

o   Secured weekly coverage in community newspapers, major dailies, and on radio and television.

o   Increased both employer participation and job placement in city-sponsored campaign for summer jobs.

EDUCATION

M.B.A., *Finance and International Business*, New York University, 1985

B.A., *Communications*, University of Minnesota, 1976

Meg Thompson
234 Washington Street, Apt. 22
Brooklyn, NY 11218
(718) 138-5522

OBJECTIVE	Market Director for an information, financial services company.
SUMMARY	Experienced in all phases of marketing information: sales and market research; merger and acquisition analysis; public and press relations; financial analysis; government affairs.

EXPERIENCE

Information Systems, Inc.   **1/92 to present**
Manager, Data Products

Was hired by former manager to market high-speed datafeeds and data base products to domestic and international financial service firms.

- Define product positioning and strategy; develop business plan and financial projections for pricing analyses and sales forecasts.

- Manage all aspects of product development and release process, including product design, testing and evaluation, product introduction and roll-out.

- Identify market opportunities and target sales prospects for product promotion; create marketing brochures, direct mail campaigns and other sales materials;

- Initiate sales contacts and generate leads; train sales force and sales support staff to identify sales opportunities; establish sales incentives.

Financial Systems   **5/89 to 1/91**
Manager, Customer Relations and Promotional Services

When Datanet was acquired by Financial Systems, I was retained by Financial Systems to develop and direct all sales promotion programs, special events and trade show exhibitions for their domestic business.

- Exhibited services successfully at more than 115 customer sales meetings, financial conferences and industry trade shows during 1991; increased conference and show exhibits by 30% without increasing operational expenses.

- Orchestrated annual sales conference and other special events; planned and managed program budgets; contracted with vendors; designed programs and selected speakers.

Datanet   **5/87 to 5/89**
Manager, Sales and Marketing

Was hired as President's assistant and managed all marketing and marketing communications to promote company and services to institutional market.

- Coordinated special projects, including all phases of $1.5 million expansion of institutional sales and trading area; directed project planning, budgeting, facilities renovation, vendor contracts, system testing and user training.

- Initiated sales campaign to increase soft dollar commitments; arranged participation in investment conferences, security analyst meetings, and trade shows; created sales promotion materials and developed monthly newsletter for institutional customers.

- Managed press contacts; prepared all press releases and executive speeches.

General Products   1/86 to 5/87
Senior Financial Analyst

Consolidated and analyzed financial results for manufacturing division, reporting to financial controller.

- Corporate liaison to 25 regional plant controllers to ensure accurate and timely financial reporting; designed and implemented PC-based financial package to facilitate consolidation of monthly statements.

- Booked division's monthly, quarterly and annual earnings, taxes and depreciation to corporate accounts; analyzed results.

Business Advisors, Inc.   8/83 to 1/86
Volunteer Consultant

U.S. Information Agency   8/80 to 8/83
Foreign Service Information Officer

Promoted U.S. foreign policy to journalists, government officials and advisors, and other opinion leaders.

- Organized seminars, conferences and cultural events sponsored by the U.S. Embassy or affiliated cultural and exchange organizations.

- Managed local media relations, initiating contact for press placement, interviews with embassy officials, or background briefings; supervised press and publications staff.

City of Minneapolis   10/78 to 8/80
Public Affairs Specialist

Publicized and promoted successful programs of city agency.

- Secured weekly coverage in community newspapers, major dailies, and on radio and television.

- Increased both employer participation and job placement in city-sponsored campaign for summer jobs.

EDUCATION

M.B.A., *Finance and International Business,* New York University, 1985

B.A., *Communications,* University of Minnesota, 1976

important piece of data for each of her six positions—in her "after" resume as well as in the "before" version. If you can't see what it is, turn to page 164.

SAMPLE RESUMES FOR A SLIGHT CAREER CHANGE

For those of you interested in changing your career direction a little, the trick is to make your new universe of prospective employers as comfortable with you as you would like to be with them. For this to happen you must talk their language, arranging your accomplishments and skills in such a way that a new boss can easily visualize you as a member of the team.

On the following pages are the resumes of three job seekers with career change on their mind, who have done a good job of achieving an early step toward their goal. Adapt from their tactics what you can:

Claims Investigator

Robert Lencioni has put in seven productive years as a revenue officer with the IRS, but believes his future lies in the private sector. His Summary and Experience Highlights emphasize all of the attributes that many corporations in the financial arena would prize. (See pages 153–154.)

TV Writer/Producer

Pamela Black's dream from the age of nine has been to be a television producer. For a while she thought the only way to get into the profession was from the business side. Even as a TV instructor in the Rochester, NY, School District, she pursued a business degree on the side. Now she has 20 years in the field, with several awards, artistic contributions, and creative accomplishments to help her make the transition. (See pages 155–156.)

Musical Consultant

Stan Christodlous is a successful jazz and classical musician with enviable arranging and composing credits. His problem is that although he enjoys his work, his family life is suffering because most of his playing dates last until well after midnight. This gives

ROBERT O. LENCIONI   91-48 79 Road, Apt. 6G Woodhaven, NY 11421   (718) 441-6620

OBJECTIVE: INVESTIGATOR   --   CLAIMS / COLLECTIONS
              To apply in-depth experience with highly sophisticated collection and
              investigation procedures on behalf of corporate financial institution

SUMMARY: Seven years experience with Internal Revenue Service as officer in charge
              of investigation and resolution of business and personal tax problems.
              In-depth understanding of business, including collection, investigation,
              interviewing and bookeeping procedures. Knowledge of computer programming.
              Capable adminstrator and supervisor of personnel. Skills transferrable to corporate
              application.

HIGHLIGHTS OF EXPERIENCE:

1988 to   INTERNAL REVENUE SERVICE
Present   New York, NY
              Revenue Officer
              Charged with independent responsibility for investigation and deter-
              mination of tax claims against large accounts ($50,000 or more) with
              full authority to resolve problems
              * Perform complex credit analyses in connection with tax liens,
                 collateral agreements and uncollectable accounts
              * Conduct intensive investigations of large corporations and prominent
                 high-income individuals to uncover hidden assets, analyze financial
                 condition and determine valuation of properties
              * Maintain comprehensive and practical knowledge of current collection
                 techniques including
                 -- Laws on rights of creditors
                 -- Forced assessment and collection
                 -- Lien priorities and bankruptcies
                 -- Summons procedures
                 -- Interpretation of public records
                 -- Application of such laws and procedure in extremely complex and
                     often delicate situations
              * Originated new techniques and creative approaches in application of
                 general tax and collection guidelines
              * Developed keen ability to influence, motivate, interview and educate
                 persons who are generally fearful and uncooperative, through use of
                 sophisticated interpersonal skills
              * Assist taxpayers in understanding of regulations; negotiate payment
                 schedules to fulfill obligations
              * Serve as technical expert in matters before the tax court
              * Serve as classroom instructor in training of IRS personnel; evaulate
                 courses and recommend changes
              * Received steady promotion to highest level in job category

1984   DEPARTMENT OF SOCIAL SERVICES
  to   New York, NY
1988

              Caseworker
              * Investigated and assisted people on welfare
                 - Determined need for assistance and made recommendations
              * Worked independently in the field

MILITARY: United States Army, West Germany
              1982-84 - Personnel and Adminstrative Specialist (Spec/5)

EDUCATION: St. John's University, Jamaica, NY
1981 - BA, Social Sciences
1985 - Graduate School (courses in Accounting, Statistics
                       Business Management)

Control Data Institute, New York, NY
1986-88 - courses in Computer Programming (FORTRAN, COBOL)

PAMELA BLACK   225 Wilkinson Street, #8-B   Home   402-755-0434
                           Omaha, Nebraska 68028   Work   402-474-1029

OBJECTIVE   TV WRITING/PRODUCING/DIRECTING -- Commercial, cable, public or
                                                 industrial television

SUMMARY   Award-winning writer/producer/director of televised programs, public service
               announcements and closed-circuit programs employing nationally known
               talent. Skilled at developing production budgets and hiring and directing creative
               staffs. Adept at designing program packages and software to fulfill specific
               client requirements.

TELEVISION EXPERIENCE

1986 to   CENTER FOR LEARNING TECHNOLOGIES, NEW YORK STATE EDUCATION
Present   DEPARTMENT, Albany, NY

               * Write, produce and direct television and closed-circuit training programs
                  for adults and children combining studio and electronic field production
                  - Administer budgets of $3,000 to $100,000
                  - Hire and direct production and creative staffs

               * Created, produced and directed award-winning, three-part media package
                  to promote good nutrition
                  - Package included 15 radio and 15 TV announcements, 30-minute public
                    TV program and 20-minute closed-circuit TV program
                  - Received medal of excellence, International Film and TV
                    Festival of New York

               * Designed, produced and implemented interactive 40-hour children's TV series
                  - Broadened and modernized curriculum through use of entertainment
                  - Positive response by students evidenced in significant learning results

               * Developed and produced ongoing statewide teleconferences
                  - Programs are "live" and broadcast by all New York State public
                    television stations
                  - Toll-free call-in provides direct answers to viewers' questions

               * Consulted with diverse school districts, providing in-service training and
                  recommending software and hardware specifications to achieve instructional
                  objectives

               * Created the "video memo" format as a way to disseminate information to staff at
                  756 locations

1978-1985   ROCHESTER CITY SCHOOL DISTRICT, Rochester, NY
              TV Instructor (1974-1975)
              Business Education Instructor (1968-1974)
              * Conceived, wrote and served as on-camera host for 42-lesson, self-instructional
                 TV series in business education used by 100 school districts statewide

                 - Wrote three manuals to accompany the series
                 - Series was telecast by public and cable TV stations and is used by the State
                   Education Department employee training center
                 - Established reputation of Rochester Televised Instruction Center and resulted in
                   further awards of contracts for videotape production
                 - Series resulted in effective replacement of classroom instruction with 79% pass
                   rate and reduction of instructional costs by almost 50%

              * Assistant Producer for five videotapes featuring the Rochester Philharmonic

EDUCATION   Syracuse University, Syracuse, NY
              1981 - MS, Business Education

              Russell Sage College, Troy, NY
              1978 - BS, Business Education
                     Graduated cum laude with high honors in Business

              University of Hawaii, Honolulu, Hawaii
              1984 - Six credits in Television Production

              Indiana University, Bloomington, Indiana
              1983 - Nine credits in Television Production
                     Awarded H. Wilson Scholarship

              New School for Social Research
              1993 - Developing Programming for Children's Television

AWARDS   Ohio State Broadcasting Award for "Visual Learning" with Gene Shalit, Walter
                 Cronkite, and Betty Furness
              International Film and Television Festival of New York Medal for "The Breakfast
                 Connection" with Lendon Smith, MD, and Marilyn Michaels

Partial list of productions available upon request

him too little time with his wife and two young children at a time in their lives when, he feels, they need him.

Stan's networking has made him aware of a need for someone with his broad-based musical and academic background to act as a consultant to publishers producing programs in his area of specialty. He is now researching and contacting appropriate executives in likely publishing houses, using the targeted resume on pages 158–159.

MULTIPLE RESUME SITUATIONS

In the following examples, the job seekers prepared a second resume for an opening somewhat different from others they had applied for. You may find some of their tactics useful as you work out your own situation. As has been the case in previous situations, identities have been changed to protect the privacy of the job seekers.

Interior Design Director

Alex Rabinowitz, an interior design director, was interested in two quite different positions, and wrote two resumes to reflect the different needs of his prospective employers.

Position #1: Alex had applied for an opening in Cleveland he had heard about; it was with a firm that had bid on and come close to (but had not been awarded) three city office landscaping contracts in the previous 14 months. Alex was so sure he was right for the job that he established residence in Cleveland, working out an arrangement with his New York employer to come into the office three days a week for the next two months. That way he could stay at his sister's apartment the other four days, establishing city contacts and setting up reconnaissance interviews. (For information on reconnaissance interviewing, see Chapter 1 of *Conquer Interview Objections*.

Although his 15-year plus years of experience had been spent exclusively in New York City (other than a two-year, part-time college position), Alex could cite a number of accomplishments and skills that made him an excellent candidate for the Cleveland job. (By spending concentrated time in that city, he was also defusing an apparent lack of familiarity for the way business was done there.)

STANLEY CHRISTODLOUS   200 East 37th Street Apt. 6A New York, NY 10016   (212) 532-4455

OBJECTIVE: Musical Consultant to a Publishing House

SUMMARY: More than 15 years experience in all phases of music: Composer, Arranger,
Conductor, Performer, Instructor and Business Manager. Compositions have
been performed in Carnegie Hall. More than ten students have become stars,
hundreds have become professional musicians and singers. Play piano and flute;
knowledgeable about all instruments.

PROFESSIONAL HIGHLIGHTS :

1990 to   NEW YORK SCHOOL OF MUSIC, New York, NY
Present

               Chairman of Music Theory Department/Instructor
               *   Instruct both graduate and undergraduate students in music theory
                         - Organized courses of study
                         - Originated new courses in Advanced Ear Training
               *   Oversee auditions for prospective applicants
               *   Recommend instructors and substitutes for hire
               *   Train new instructors
               *   Hundreds of formers students have gone on to play or sing professionally
               *   Currently in joint authorship of a music theory workbook for beginning
                    high school students in the Preparatory Division of Manhattan School of
                    Music (September, 1991 projected publication date)

Concurrent   Leader of Jazz Combo
1984 to   *   Write and arrange composition, direct appearances and perform on the piano
Present   and flute
               *   Book appearances in New York Metropolitan Areas for weddings, bar mitzvahs,
                    cocktail parties and holiday events
               *   Manage all financial affairs and arrangements for group, including billing
                    and collection

Concurrent   BROOKLYN COLLEGE, Brooklyn, NY
1985-88

               Adjunct Lecturer
               *   Taught assigned music theory and music appreciation courses to music and
                    non-music majors

1979-1987   SEAMAN'S METHODIST CHURCH, Brooklyn, NY
               Music Director

1983-1985   NEW YORK CITY COMMUNITY COLLEGE, Brooklyn, NY
               Adjunct Lecturer
               *   Taught assigned music appreciation courses to non-music majors

1975-1983   NEW YORK CITY BOARD OF EDUCATION, Brooklyn, NY
               Teacher of Orchestral Music   (1974-1977)
               *   Trained students on all orchestral instruments
               *   Instituted home use of instruments to increase interest in orchestra
               *   Developed orchestra from ten poorly trained players into well disciplined
                    musical group of 60 instrumentalists

158

General Music Teacher   (1970-1974)
* Taught music appreciation to general classes
* Trained and rehearsed school Glee Club

EDUCATION: Manhattan School of Music, New York, NY
            1982 - MM, Music Theory/Piano
                    Thesis: "Ear Training Program for College Freshman"

            New York University, New York, NY
            1980 - MA, Master of Music Education

            Howard University, Washington, DC
            1975 - BA, Music Education (cum laude)

HONORS: - Inducted into Pi Kappa Lambda, Howard University
            - Elected president of student council
            - Received Lucy E. Moten Fellowship for European study and travel - 1974
            - Achieved highest score on Regular Teacher Examination (orchestral music),
              Board of Education of New York - 1975

ORIGINAL COMPOSITIONS:
            Serenity for Solo Flute
            Theme and Variations for Piano and Bassoon
            Piano Sonata in One Movement
            Woodwind Quintet No.1
            Woodwind Quintet No.2 (performed at Carnegie Hall)
            Theme and Variation for Woodwind Quintet

MEMBER: American Music Center
            Music Theory Teachers of New York State

CERTIFIED: Music Teacher for New York State

Alex knew, for example, that his understanding of municipal codes and building department routine and bureaucracy would transfer well from New York to Cleveland, and he made sure this information was included in his Summary. (See pages 161–162.)

Position #2: Upon a recent visit home to New York City, Alex saw the following advertisement for an interior designer in *The New York Times*:

INTERIOR DESIGN
Department Head

For Tallahassee, FL ARCHITECTURAL FIRM. Position requires heavy exp in client relations, space planning, interior architectural design for hospital and/or comm'l office projects. Prof'l registration desired. Respond in confidence w/resume and salary history. T5555 TIMES 10108. All replies will be acknowledged.

The requirements fit Alex's background so well that he revised the first page of his resume, to be sure his cover letter was backed up by a resume emphasizing the hiring company's needs. His new Summary, followed by current experience thoroughly consistent with the ad copy, strengthened his case. (See page 163.)

Commercial Real Estate Broker/Financial Officer

After working his way through college and graduate school, Nick Kantzas joined a Wall Street insurance company, and several years later was hired as assistant controller by a fast-growing entrepreneurial Long Island firm. After 10 years an international conglomerate bought his company and Nick was "excessed."

After several months of unsuccessful job hunting, Nick's research—and a friend's suggestion—convinced him that he could make a career in commercial real estate. His financial background and contacts brought him two projects that he handled both efficiently and profitably. He was enthusiastic about his prospects, and in six months earned his real estate license.

At the same time he felt uneasy without a regular paycheck. As the only wage earner in the family, Nick began to think in terms of another full-time position. His solution was to spend most of his time on his job search, but also to keep an eye out for potentially profitable real estate ventures.

ALEX RABINOWITZ
417 E. 13th Street, Apt. 18D, Cleveland, Ohio 54140
(612) 935-1725

OBJECTIVE   COMMERCIAL INTERIOR DESIGN

SUMMARY: Interior designer with ten years of office landscape and residential design experience. Thorough
knowledge of trade resources. Understanding of city codes and building department routine and
bureaucracy. Comprehensive knowledge of commercial planning systems.

DESIGN EXPERIENCE:

1984 to   DANIEL STERLING, INC., New York, NY
Present   Head Designer (1985-Present)
                 Assistant Designer (1984-1985)

* Design commercial and residential spaces and direct all facets leading to completion of
projects. Supervise assistants, assuring on-schedule production of quality work. Negotiate
with architects, vendors and tradesmen, scheduling and coordinating their activities.

* Achievements

Executive business offices, Exemplar International Insurance Co., Fort Lee, NJ
The Discotheque Parfait, New York City
Rare Form contemporary restaurant, New York City
Solarium for president of Perrier Water Co.
    (featured in TOWN & COUNTRY magazine)
Private residences for leading social figures in New York City
Solarium for Richard Todd of the New York Jets, New York City

1986 to   FREE-LANCE PROJECTS
Present
* Packaging concept for Alan Fortunoff (owner of Fortunoff's), New York City

* Textile design collection for Schumacher Decorators' Walk, Riverdale Fabrics
New York City

* Kent Bragaline, New York City

* Album cover logo and publicity T-shirts for Darryl Hall and John Oates, Arista
Records, New York City

1983-1984   TABER INTERIORS, New York, NY
                 Assistant Designer

* Developed designs, conceptualization and renderings of floor plans, elevation and
layouts under tutelage of Head Designer. Coordinated design elements and
became acquainted with trends in design field.

1982-1983   BLOOMINGDALES, New York, NY
                 Designer

* Created residential interiors, utilizing existing retail product lines

1980-1982   SELF-EMPLOYED DESIGNER
              (concurrent with pursuit of MFA)

              *   Designed and conceptualized various boutiques, shopping plazas and restaurants

1977-1979   CARRIER CORPORATION, Syracuse, NY
              <u>Assistant Designer, Corporate Planning</u>

              *   Drawing, drafting, rendering

EDUCATION   COLUMBIA UNIVERSITY, New York, NY
              1988 - MFA   (GPA - 3.8/4.0)

              SYRACUSE UNIVERSITY, Syracuse, NY
              1977 - BFA, Interior Design (GPA - 4.0/4.0)
              Dean's List, eight semesters

CERTIFICATION

              Permanent Certified Design Instructor, New York State Board of Regents

ALEX RABINOWITZ
993 East 4th Street, Apt. 5C
New York, NY 10004
(212) 866-8595

OBJECTIVE: Department Head, Interior Design

SUMMARY: Commercial interior designer with 10 years management experience, including client and vendor relations. Ready to relocate.

DESIGN EXPERIENCE:

1984 to   DANIEL STERLING, INC., New York, NY
Present   Head Designer (1985-Present)
               Assistant Designer (1984-1985)

* Design commercial and residential spaces and direct all facets leading to completion of projects. Supervise assistants, assuring on-schedule production of quality work. Negotiate with architects, vendors and tradesmen, scheduling and coordinating their activities.

* Achievements

   The Discotheque Parfait, New York City
   Executive business offices, Exemplar International Insurance Co., Fort Lee, NJ
   Rare Form contemporary restaurant, New York City
   Solarium for president of Perrier Water Co.
      (featured in TOWN & COUNTRY magazine)
   Private residences for leading social figures in New York City
   Solarium for Richard Todd of the New York Jets, New York City

1986 to   FREE-LANCE PROJECTS
Present
* Packaging concept for Alan Fortunoff (owner of Fortunoff's), New York City

* Textile design collection for Schumacher Decorators' Walk, Riverdale Fabrics
     New York City

* Kent Bragaline, New York City

* Album cover logo and publicity T-shirts for Darryl Hall and John Oates, Arista
     Records, New York City

* Skating Club set and costume design - Utica Figure Skating Club, Clinton Figure
     Skating Club, Hamilton Figure Skating Club, Ice Club of Syracuse

Reproduced here are Nick's real estate-oriented resume, followed by a resume he modified for job opportunities similar to the one he held before his downsizing. (The version you see here was prepared for a chief financial officer opening in a small software company, with crossover responsibilities for marketing, sales, and manufacturing.)

See Appendix B of *Conquer Interview Objections*, for additional examples of resumes written for specific situations.

Answer to Question on Page 152: Meg Thompson failed to include locations for six of her seven employers. (The seventh, a city government department, was self-evident.)

Take Stock of Your Situation

This ends *Conquer Resume Objections*. If you've gotten as far as this page, we assume you've found some answers in one or more of the career problem areas listed below:

1. Defining your specific career problem
2. Pinpointing your career direction
3. Organizing your job search
4. Developing a marketing plan
5. Writing your master resume and cover letter
6. Overcoming resume objections

If you need assistance in the following areas, you'll find it in *Conquer Interview Objections*:

1. Reconnaissance strategy for targeted companies
2. Making the best interview first impression
3. Becoming the ideal candidate
4. Testing for predictable interview objections
5. Overcoming camouflaged interview objections
6. Asking for the job; negotiating the best compensation
7. Flourishing on your next job

If there are aspects of your particular situation that have not been covered to your satisfaction, please write to tell us, so we can address them in the next edition. If you have suggestions for other topics that you would like to see covered, please let us know.

NICHOLAS KANTZAS
74 Iceland Drive
Huntington, Long Island
New York   11743

516-842-1437 - Home
516-844-1414 - Office

OBJECTIVE: Commercial real estate management and development.

SUMMARY: Versatile executive with breadth of practical experience in financial planning, data processing, legal, and construction issues involved in real estate and general business development.

RECENT REAL ESTATE PROJECTS

- Organized the Hale Site Condominium and Yacht Club in an effort to preserve an historic beach front from industrial development. This required negotiating the purchase of the property for $45 million, formulating a business plan to secure financing, and marketing the sale of 150 living units and 100 moorings and lockers.

- Active in local and state wide civic affairs as Delegate to the Long Island Sound Assembly, former Treasurer of the Hale Site Civic Association and member of Huntington Planning and Zoning Board.

1976-1986   **McCormick Enterprises**

Controller   1980-1986

- Worked with Sales, Marketing, and Manufacturing, to formulate the first five year plan for McCormick.

- Through reorganization, automation, and redefinition of responsibilities, was able to maintain the same size staff in spite of a sales growth of $500 million.

Assistant Controller   1975-1980

- Developed annual audit plans for the Audit Committee of the Board of Directors.

- Developed the audit priority model to insure adequate coverage and external audit coordination worldwide. (This approach was the subject of an article published in the "Financial Executive".)

- Thirty Internal Auditors I hired, representing 65% of the total, were recruited for financial positions within the company.

- Led Seminars for Directors of Internal Audit on behalf of the Institute of Internal Auditors.

1969-1975   **American Worldwide Enterprises**

Assistant General Auditor

- Supervised twenty-five internal auditors around the world.

MILITARY

U.S. Naval Reserve, Honorable Discharge 1970.

EDUCATION

Fordham University, B.B.A. Economics 1967

Fordham Business School; 1969

Real Estate Sales License; 1987

NICHOLAS KANTZAS
74 Iceland Drive
Huntington, Long Island
New York 11743

516-842-1437 - Home
516-844-1414 - Office

OBJECTIVE: Chief Financial Officer

SUMMARY: Versatile financial executive with a breadth of practical experience in business planning, data processing, auditing, acquisitions and real estate.

1976-1986 **McCormick Enterprises**

Controller 1980-1986

- Worked with Sales, Marketing, and Manufacturing, to formulate the first five-year plan for McCormick.

- Through reorganization, automation, and redefinition of responsibilities, was able to maintain the same size staff in spite of a sales growth of $500 million.

Assistant Controller 1975-1980

- Developed annual audit plans for the Audit Committee of the Board of Directors.

- Developed the audit priority model to insure adequate coverage and external audit coordination worldwide. (This approach was the subject of an article published in the "Financial Executive".)

- Thirty Internal Auditors I hired, representing 65% of the total, were recruited for financial positions within the company.

- Led Seminars for Directors of Internal Audit on behalf of the Institute of Internal Auditors.

1969-1975 **American Worldwide Enterprises**

Assistant General Auditor

- Supervised twenty-five internal auditors around the world.

RECENT REAL ESTATE PROJECTS

- Organized the Hale Site Condominium and Yacht Club in an effort to preserve an historic beach front from industrial development. This required negotiating the purchase of the property for $45 million, formulating a business plan to secure financing, and marketing the sale of 150 living units and 100 moorings and lockers.

- Active in local and state wide civic affairs as Delegate to the Long Island Sound Assembly, former Treasurer of the Hale Site Civic Association and member of Huntington Planning and Zoning Board.

MILITARY

U.S. Naval Reserve, Honorable Discharge 1970.

EDUCATION

Fordham University, B.B.A. Economics 1967

Fordham Business School; 1969

Real Estate Sales License; 1987

ADDITIONAL READING

Chapman, Elwood N. *Attitude: Your Most Priceless Possession*. Los Altos, CA: Crisp Publications, Inc., 1987 How to stay positive in a time of considerable stress, by the author of "Your Attitude is Showing," a million-copy seller.

James, Muriel. *Born to Win: Transactional Analysis With Gestalt Experiments*. New York: Penguin Books USA, Inc., 1978. Every person has the potential to be a winner, a responsive, fulfilled human being. A guide for self-discovery and growth to help increase your awareness of the power to direct your life and enhance the lives of others.

Waitley, Denis. *Seeds of Greatness: The Ten Best Kept Secrets of Total Success*. New York: Pocket Books, 1984. How to combine positive attitudes with your natural aptitudes or abilities to change your lifestyle, choose goals, be a self manager.

Reasons for Unemployment Compensation Benefit Disqualification[1]

Even though you've worked long enough and earned sufficient wages to be eligible for unemployment benefits, you may be disqualified for other reasons. In most states you are disqualified from receiving benefits if you:

1. Quit your job without a sufficient work-related cause (Leaving your job because your spouse was transferred out of the area is not a sufficient cause to quit that would allow you to collect benefits in most states.) Warning: Heated discussions and actions in termination interviews can often supply critical evidence of whether you quit or were constructively discharged.

2. Were discharged for "repeated willful misconduct," the most common causes of which are:

- Chronic absence from work, particularly if you give no plausible reason
- Excessive tardiness, without good reason
- Violation of workplace rules (if the rules are reasonable, you knew about them, and your violation was intentional)
- Fighting, which can also qualify as "just cause" if it seriously endangers someone's life or safety. (Unlike willful misconduct, just cause requires only one incident.)

---

[1]Lewin, G. Joel III, *Every Employee's Guide to the Law*, (New York: Pantheon Books, 1993), 271–279.

- Profanity, depending on the type of workplace. (For example, being fired for profanity on a construction site probably wouldn't disqualify you from receiving unemployment benefits.)
- Sleeping on the job

Alcoholism or Drug Addiction: Most states treat alcohol or drug addiction as an illness. Therefore, if your employer fires you for repeatedly using drugs or alcohol on the job, you may still be eligible for unemployment benefits. You may have to document your addiction with medical evidence supplied by the physician who is treating you.

3. Are discharged for "just cause." Most state laws take the position that an employer shouldn't have to tolerate behavior at work that endangers his property or the health or safety of others, nor should he have to pay unemployment benefits for someone who was fired for such a "just cause."

So you may be disqualified from receiving unemployment benefits if your actions are flagrant enough to give your employer just cause to fire you, even if you did it only once. Examples might be fighting on the job (if the fight is violent enough or actually causes injury) or intentionally destroying your employer's property.

4. Are fired for committing a felony in the course of your employment, or for larceny of property or some type of service (like the phone company employee who hooked herself into "free" phone service)—also in the course of your employment. Most states place a minimum value on the property or service that is stolen for the theft to disqualify you from unemployment benefits.

5. Are fired for taking part in an illegal strike. (Note: If an employer simply closes his doors because of a contract dispute, or won't allow you to work until the dispute is settled, or says you can work only if you agree to work for less money, more hours, or under worse conditions than you were working before the dispute began, this is considered a *lockout,* and you are eligible to receive unemployment benefits.)

6. Are serving a prison sentence. (Most states set a minimum sentence, such as thirty days, for you to be ineligible for benefits.)

7. Are a teacher between terms or a professional athlete between seasons and have reasonable assurance of returning for the next term or season.

8.   Voluntarily retire. Note: If you are forced to retire because of your age, you may still be eligible to receive benefits. (You may also have an age discrimination case. Consult an attorney, or read Chapter 5 of *Every Employee's Guide to the Law*.)

B

Current Minimum and Maximum Weekly Unemployment Benefit Amount, By State*

State	Minimum Weekly Benefit Amount	Maximum Weekly Benefit Amount	Duration Weeks	Maximum Potential Benefit Amount
Alabama	$22	$165	26	$3,120
Alaska	44	284	26[†]	4,888
Arizona	40	185	26	3,510
Arkansas	43	240	26	5,096
California	40	230	26[†]	4,316
Colorado	25	250	26	5,538
Connecticut	15	356	26[†]	4,992
Delaware	20	245	26	5,330
District of Columbia	50	335	26[†]	6,500
Florida	10	250	26	4,550

*U.S. Dept. of Labor statistics as of 1993

[†]Does not include possible extension of benefits for an additional year. Policy varies from state to state.

State	Minimum Weekly Benefit Amount	Maximum Weekly Benefit Amount	Duration Weeks	Maximum Potential Benefit Amount
Georgia	37	185	26	3,770
Hawaii	5	322	26†	5,220
Idaho	44	223	26	4,810
Illinois	51	300	26	4,186
Indiana	50	181	26	2,496
Iowa	30	245	26	4,108
Kansas	59	239	26	5,122
Kentucky	22	217	26	3,640
Louisiana	10	181	26	5,330
Maine	35	297	26	3,952
Maryland	25	223	26	5,070
Massachusetts	14	468	30	6,600
Michigan	42	293	26	5,122
Minnesota	38	279	26	6,214
Mississippi	30	165	26	3,380
Missouri	45	175	26	3,250
Montana	52	209	26	4,446
Nebraska	20	154	26	3,276
Nevada	16	217	26	4,446
New Hampshire	32	188	26	3,900
New Jersey	69	325	26	5,564
New Mexico	38	191	26	4,004
New York	40	300	26	4,680
North Carolina	22	267	26	4,784
North Dakota	43	212	26	5,122
Ohio	42	300	26	3,822
Oklahoma	16	229	26†	3,560
Oregon	63	271	26†	4,516

State	Minimum Weekly Benefit Amount	Maximum Weekly Benefit Amount	Duration Weeks	Maximum Potential Benefit Amount
Pennsylvania	35	325	26	6,032
Puerto Rico	7	133	20†	1,900
Rhode Island	41	367	30	5,730
South Carolina	20	125	26	3,250
South Dakota	28	129	26	3,354
Tennessee	30	125	26	3,250
Texas	40	210	26	5,460
Utah	14	197	26	5,122
Vermont	25	154	26	4,004
Virginia	65	167	26	4,342
Washington	68	197	30	5,910
West Virginia	24	225	26	5,850
Wisconsin	4	196	26	5,096
Wyoming	4	192	26	5,148

C

Managing Your Money

Money is important at any time, but in your current situation, it matters even more. Don't resist taking a hard look at your budget. Knowing the realities will reduce your anxiety.
This exercise may take several hours to complete. Before you begin, gather all your financial records and documents, several sharp pencils, and an eraser.

INCOME

A. *Lump-sum Income*

Severance pay	$ _____
Vacation pay	$ _____
Cash on hand	$ _____
Savings	$ _____
Tax refund	$ _____
Pension contribution	$ _____
Other _____	$ _____
_____	$ _____
_____	$ _____
_____	$ _____
_____	$ _____
Total	$ _____

B. *Continuing Income (Calculate Monthly)*

Unemployment compensation $ _____

Spouse's income (net after taxes) $ _____

Union benefits $ _____

Alimony/child support $ _____

Part-time job $ _____

Dividends $ _____

Rental income $ _____

Other _____ $ _____

_____ $ _____

_____ $ _____

_____ $ _____

_____ $ _____

Total $ _____

C. *Calculate Monthly Income*

1. Divide lump-sum income total (A) by 3 $ _____
   Add continuing monthly income (B) $ _____
   Total (If I find a job in 3 months; we
   have a potential monthly income of:) $ _____

2. Divide lump-sum income total (A) by 6 $ _____
   Add continuing monthly income (B) $ _____
   Total (If I find a job in 6 months,
   we have a potential monthly income of:) $ _____

3. Divide lump-sum income total (A) by 9 $ _____
   Add continuing monthly income (B) $ _____
   Total (If I find a job in 9 months, we
   have a potential monthly income of:) $ _____

4. Divide lump-sum income total (A) by 12 $ _____
   Add continuing monthly income (B) $ _____
   Total (If I find a job in 12 months,
   we have a potential monthly income of:) $ _____

D. *Estimate Needed Income*

At this point, my best judgment is that it will take me _____ months to find a job.

If you make less than $40,000 per year, add 3 months to that estimate. If you make more than $40,000 per year, add 6 months to that estimate.

Divide lump-sum income by your estimate,
plus safety factor of 3 or 6 $ _____

Add continuing monthly income $ _____

Subtract benefits that may expire $ _____

     Total $ _____

E. *Potential Supplementary Income*

Sales of stock/bonds $ _____

Sale of property (boat, second home) $ _____

Paid-up insurance (loan value) $ _____

Second mortgage $ _____

Other Loan (family, etc.) $ _____

EXPENSES

Fill in your average monthly expenses in the following chart. If you can't calculate the average, use last month's figures.

Rent or mortgage _____	Doctors/Dentists O.V. _____
Property tax _____	Medicine _____
Heat _____	Clothes _____
	Subtotal _____
Gas _____	Dry cleaning/laundry _____
Electricity_____	Tuition _____
Water _____	School books/supp._____
Sewerage _____	Childcare _____

Garbage _____

Telephone _____

Home Maint. _____

Property ins. _____

Car payment(s) _____

Auto insurance _____

Gas/Oil _____

Repair/main. _____

License/regist. _____

Public transp. _____

Tolls/parking _____

Groceries _____

Food away from home _____

Life insurance _____

Hospitalization _____

Books/Newspapers/
Magazines _____

Entertainment/
Hobbies _____

Gifts/Holidays _____

Cigarettes _____

Liquor _____

Beauty salon/Barber _____

Alimony/Child support _____

Charitable contrib. _____

Credit card debt _____

Savings _____

Other _____

_____

_____

_____

_____

Total Monthly Expenses _____

Total Projected Monthly
Income (from page 178) _____

If your expenses are less than your monthly income, you're in good shape; if they are more than your monthly income, continue on to Appendix D.

D

Plan for Cutting Expenses

Take a realistic look at what you can save by cutting back on some of your living expenses. Enter the amount of money you can save and how you intend to do it in the following chart.

Expenditure	Amount I Can Save	How I Can Save It
Rent or Mortgage		
Property tax		
Heat		
Gas		
Electricity		
Water		
Sewerage		
Garbage		
Telephone		
Home maintenance		
Property insurance		
Car payment(s)		
Auto insurance		
Gas/Oil		
Repairs/Maintenance		
License/Registration		

Public Transportation _____ _____

Tolls/Parking _____ _____

Groceries _____ _____

Food Away From Home _____ _____

Life Insurance _____ _____

Hospitalization _____ _____

Doctor/Dentist O.V. _____ _____

Medicine _____ _____

Clothes _____ _____

Cleaning/Laundry _____ _____

Tuition _____ _____

School Books/Supplies _____ _____

Child Care _____ _____

Books/Newspapers/Mags. _____ _____

Entertainment/Hobbies _____ _____

Gifts/Holidays _____ _____

Cigarettes _____ _____

Liquor _____ _____

Beauty Salon/Barber Shop _____ _____

Alimony/Child support _____ _____

Charitable Contributions _____ _____

Credit Card Debt _____ _____

Savings _____ _____

Other _____ _____

Total Estimated Savings
Revised Total Monthly
Expenses _____
(Total Monthly Expenses
from page 180 minus Total
Estimated Savings)

Projected Total Monthly   _____
Income
(From page 178)

If your expenses are still larger than your income, you will need to take a closer look at Potential Supplementary Income (Page 179) in order to make up the shortfall. Write your plan in the space below selling some of your assets or taking loans.

What

_____

_____

_____

_____

_____

How Much

_____

_____

_____

_____

_____

When

_____

_____

_____

_____

_____

If your income and expenses still don't balance, you need to use an even sharper pencil. Take a harder look at expenses, be more creative in thinking about part-time job possibilities for everyone in the family, and start making appointments tomorrow to renegotiate some of your debts and monthly payment obligations.

Many people who complete this "Plan for Cutting Expenses" exercise will feel better: Merely knowing the reality of your financial situation should ease much of your anxiety. Others, however, will feel depressed, especially when income and expenses don't come quickly into line. If you are in the latter category, get up from your desk and do some physical exercise—now. Come back to the problem later with a clear mind. You will find the answers.

E

What Kind of Boss Are You?

It used to be that an ideal boss had to be a hard-driving autocrat. Today, as you may remember from Chapter 2, there is another breed of manager who is both respected and gets the job done.

Marjorie Schiller, President of the management consulting firm Schiller & Associates, has devised a test to help evaluate your method of managing. For each situation below, circle the response that most closely approximates the way you would react.

Keep in mind that there are no correct or incorrect answers. When you've completed all 10 statements, take a reading on your response from the key on page 188–189.

1. Your personnel department sends out a memo announcing a new company policy that you and many other employees aren't too keen on. One of your subordinates, who also happens to be a close friend, tells you that the memo confirms what he's suspected all along: Personnel departments are a nuisance—and this one really earns a blue ribbon for officiousness. Your response:
   a. This would never happen because none of your subordinates takes such liberties. Besides, you don't believe in getting chummy with the people you work with.
   b. "You're right. This is definitely one of the more ridiculous policies they've come up with. Just forget about it."
   c. "Sure, I have a few concerns about this memo, but it's not worth fighting."
   d. "This policy is intended to help company performance, so let's just try to adjust to it."

2. An employee you've always been able to count on is going through a divorce. Because of legal and emotional problems, his work standards have slipped considerably. You:

a. Say nothing. After all, he's earned a few goodwill points, and there are times when you have to take people's feelings into account.

b. Tell him you understand what he's going through but that he still has to pull his weight.

c. Remind him that he's a key performer in your department and that if he doesn't shape up, the accuracy of his work could suffer further.

d. Tell him you won't let his personal problems interfere with work.

3. Two people on your staff who now have cubicles are making equal claims to an office that's just been vacated. You:

a. Tell them to draw straws for it; it's the fairest and least disruptive solution.

b. Tell them you'll make a decision shortly and pray that something comes up soon that'll help you make up your mind.

c. Have a frank discussion with both employees to determine which one will be most upset by losing out. Then give the office to that person.

d. Give in to the squeakiest wheel.

4. You have skimpier funds than usual for staff raises this year. You decide to:

a. Divide the money equally, so everyone's at least a little bit happier.

b. Carefully calculate raises based on people's performance and contributions.

c. Divide the money among your top performers. Give the others nothing.

d. Give token raises to your best people and no pay increase to anyone else. That way, you'll have more flexibility to invest in top-priority projects.

5. One of your staff members has been doing things the same way for 10 years. His projects are always successful, and there's no reason for him to change. But your boss is expecting major reforms in your department, and you know you're being judged on your ability to turn things around. You say to your subordinate:

a. "You've been operating this way for 10 years. Damn it, it's time to change."

b. "I'd be interested in hearing any new ideas you have for your projects."
c. "The boss is breathing down my neck to make some changes. We'd better come up with something—quick."
d. "I've researched your area carefully and I'd like to get your opinion on some new ideas I have for your projects."

6. You're beginning to get flak because a number of your people routinely arrive late. But you've been overlooking their tardiness because your staff produces top-notch work and puts in substantial overtime. You send a memo to the executive committee, saying:
   a. They should overlook the tardiness of your staff because of the excellent job everyone's been doing.
   b. Your staff's productivity is 20 percent higher than the company average, so tardiness isn't the issue.
   c. Old habits die hard, but in the interest of company policy, you'll ask your people to show up on time.
   d. You've already told your people that you don't approve of their crawling in at 9:30 and that anyone who can't get in on time from now on will be penalized.

7. There's a company-wide crackdown, and all employees must arrive by 9:00 A.M. So you call a staff meeting and say:
   a. "I want you all in here by 9:00—no ifs, ands, or buts."
   b. "I know 9:00 A.M. is a little early for some of you, but 10:00 is really too late. So why don't we shoot for . . ."
   c. "I know you all stay late and take work home, but the company does have regulations. So I'm afraid you're going to have to come in earlier."
   d. "Let's come in earlier for a few weeks to get them off our backs. Then, we'll be able to go back to our usual routine."

8. You tried—but failed—to negotiate an above-average merit increase for a subordinate who's a loyal and steady performer. Though she seems to have plateaued in her current role, you like her and very much want her to stay. What should you do?
   a. To make her feel better, you tell her that she'll probably get a substantial raise next year.
   b. Tell her that the two of you will have to come up with some new responsibilities for her so you can finagle a bigger raise.

   c. You say, "I'm sorry, but you're doing basically the same job you were doing a year ago, and according to company policy, I can't give you the raise you'd like."

   d. You say nothing. You figure she doesn't have the gumption to confront you or the initiative to start a job search.

9. You've been told that your department has two weeks to develop a new program for one of your clients. But you know your people will have to work virtually around the clock to pull it together that quickly. You tell your boss:

   a. "That's not enough time to get the job done, and I can't ask my people to sacrifice so much of their personal time."

   b. "We can't do an outstanding job in just two weeks. But if you can give us more time, even a few more days, we'll have a better shot at it."

   c. "One way or another, I'm sure my team will come through on this, no matter what the sacrifice."

   d. "Even if I have to crack a few heads, we'll get the job done."

10. Let's assume you promise your boss you'll get the new program going in two weeks. Now you tell your staff:

   a. "I wish we had more time, but you know how critical this project is to the company. So let's all pitch in and do the best we can."

   b. "I think that if we sit down and map out a way to streamline the process, we'll get the job done on time."

   c. "Hey, folks. We know I'm on the line with this project. So I'm going to have to rely on each of you to help me out."

   d. "I don't want to hear any bellyaching. You all knew what you were getting into when you took the job. So if you can't take the heat, get out of the kitchen."

Self-Evaluation

This test is adapted from research by behavioral scientist Elias Porter, who found that executives generally have one of these four basic management styles: the Driver, the Thinker, the Friend, and the Visionary. Read the descriptions below, then pick the one you think best describes the kind of boss you are. The scoring instructions that follow will help you determine how accurate you are.

THE DRIVER. People describe you as a "can-do" person, a tireless taskmaster. You do whatever's necessary to get the job done, even if it means riding roughshod over people's feelings. Sure you're tough, but you get results.

Potential Weakness: In your single-minded devotion to getting the job done, you may be overly demanding and insensitive to others. Your subordinates may consider you unjust.

THE THINKER. You think everything through so methodically that you rarely make a false move. You like detail and precision, and you've gained respect for your meticulous planning and accuracy. Above all, though, you're a strongly principled person who believes in being fair with your employees. And to avoid favoritism, you're careful to keep your professional and private lives entirely separate.

Potential weakness: Your concern for detail can be interpreted as quibbling and nit-picking by others. And this tendency toward perfectionism can trip you up when you have to make a quick decision.

THE FRIEND. Protecting your people and planning for their personal growth is your overriding responsibility. For that reason, you go to great lengths to understand people's needs and avoid stepping on anyone's toes.

Potential weakness: There's the danger that in putting so much emphasis on people's feelings you end up neglecting the bottom-line responsibilities of your job. In your desire to promote departmental harmony, you sometimes back down from necessary confrontations.

THE VISIONARY. You use a blend of styles, adapting your response to the situation. But no matter what you do, you always have the overall welfare of the team at heart. You're open-minded, flexible, and an avid company networker.

Potential weakness: Your adaptability could be construed by others as unpredictability. You also have the tendency to assume—somewhat naively—that others share your enthusiasm and are just as willing to make personal sacrifices for the good of the company.

Answer Key

Using the key on the next page, see how many answers you had for Driver (D), Thinker (T), Friend (F), and Visionary (V). Enter your score in the space provided. Your highest score indicates your favored style as a boss.

1. a-T,	b-D,	c-F,	d-V
2. a-F,	b-V,	c-T,	d-D
3. a-T,	b-V,	c-F,	d-D
4. a-F,	b-T,	c-D,	d-V
5. a-D,	b-F,	c-V,	d-T
6. a-F,	b-T,	c-V,	d-D
7. a-D,	b-F,	c-T,	d-V
8. a-F,	b-V,	c-T,	d-D
9. a-F,	b-T,	c-V,	d-D
10. a-V,	b-T,	c-F,	d-D

Driver (D) _____   Thinker (T) _____

Friend (F) _____   Visionary (V) _____

See Chapter 2 of *Conquer Interview Objections* for a look at the four personality types as interviewers.

F

List of Action Verbs

The following list will help you identify verbs that reflect your job responsibilities or accomplishments. Use them in your resume as appropriate.

Preside	Report	Consider	Reconcile
Govern	Contact	Select	Update
Direct	Communicate	Revise	Upgrade
Administer	Service	Require	Arrange
Manage	Meet	Review	Modify
Supervise	Seek	Compare	Follow-through
Control	Declare	Translate	Distribute
Execute	Promote	Justify	Sort
Authorize	Arrange	Interpret	Correct
Assume	Write	Appraise	Audit
Decide	Inform	Rectify	Account
Negotiate	Publicize	Implement	Collect
Represent	Persuade	Set up	Credit
Program	Harmonize	Maintain	Synthesize
Recruit	Moderate	Procure	Compute
Interview	Approve	Extend	Insure
Counsel	Disapprove	Anticipate	Secure
Guide	Appropriate	Forecast	Safeguard
Conduct	Contract	Render	Protect
Screen	Strengthen	Furnish	Store
Engage	Produce	Provide	Accept
Assign	Improve	Propose	Adhere
Delegate	Acquire	Prepare	Manipulate
Stimulate	Return	Recommend	Reshape
Train	Discharge	Test	Make

Teach	Disburse	Handle	Exercise
Motivate	Establish	Transfer	Design
Enhance	Conceive	Supply	Create
Process	Initiate	Issue	Invent
Enlarge	Plan	Submit	Research
Requisition	Organize	Receive	Activate
Ship	Operate	Reclaim	Formulate
Instruct	Allocate	Release	Develop
Terminate	Schedule	Systematize	Coordinate
Assist	Investigate	Index	Perform
Cooperate	Identify	Compile	Change
Serve	Define	Catalogue	Compose
Participate	Evaluate	Analyze	Continue
Employ	Measure	Examine	Expand
Contribute	Determine	Summarize	

G

Where the Jobs Are—And Will Be

Grouped here are all the jobs employing more than 150,000 in this country—about 90 percent of all U.S. workers—and the growth that the Bureau of Labor Statistics calculates for each. Does your job have a future? If not, maybe you'd better think about an alternative.

	Jobs in Thousands 1990	Projected Growth 1990 to 2005
Executive, Administrative, and Managerial		
General managers & top executives	3,100	14 to 24%
Accountants & auditors	985	25 to 34%
Financial managers	701	25 to 34%
Other managers	701	N.A.
Restaurant & food service managers	557	25 to 34%
Personnel & labor relations managers	456	25 to 34%
Marketing, advertising & PR managers	427	35% or more
Wholesale & retail buyers	361	14 to 24%
Education administrators	348	14 to 24%
Engineering & data-processing managers	315	25 to 34%
Purchasing agents & managers	300	14 to 24%
Health services managers	257	35% or more
Property & real estate managers	225	25 to 34%
Administrative service managers	221	14 to 24%
Inspectors & compliance officers	216	25 to 34%
Industrial production managers	210	14 to 24%
Construction contractors & managers	183	25 to 34%
Cost estimators	173	14 to 24%

	Jobs in Thousands 1990	Projected Growth 1990 to 2005
Loan officers & counselors	172	25 to 34%
Management analysts & consultants	151	35% or more

Marketing and Sales

Retail sales workers	4,754	25 to 34%
Cashiers	2,633	25 to 34%
Manufacturers' & wholesale sales reps	1,944	14 to 24%
Service sales representatives	588	35% or more
Insurance agents & brokers	439	14 to 24%
Real estate agents, brokers & appraisers	413	14 to 24%
Counter & retail clerks	215	25 to 34%
Securities & financial serv. sales reps	191	35% or more

Professional

Registered nurses	1,727	35% or more
Kindergarten & elementary teachers	1,520	14 to 24%
Engineers	1,519	25 to 34%
Secondary school teachers	1,280	25 to 34%
Other professionals	865	N.A.
College & university faculty	712	14 to 24%
Lawyers & judges	633	25 to 34%
Social & human service workers	583	25 to 34%
Physicians	580	25 to 34%
Adult education teachers	517	25 to 34%
Computer system analysts	463	35% or more
Physical, speech & other therapists	382	25% to 34%
Musicians & other performing artists	356	14 to 24%
Designers	339	25 to 34%
Ministers, priests & rabbis	312	14 to 24%
Architects & surveyors	236	14 to 24%
Reporters, announcers & PR specialists	233	14 to 24%
Writers & editors	232	14 to 24%
Visual artists	230	25 to 34%
Social scientists	224	35% or more
Coaches & sports instructors	221	14 to 24%
Recreation workers	194	14 to 24%

	Jobs in Thousands 1990	Projected Growth 1990 to 2005
Dentists	174	5 to 13%
Pharmacists	169	14 to 24%
Physical scientists	157	14 to 24%

Transportation and Material Moving

Truck drivers	2,700	14 to 24%
Other transportation workers	698	5 to 13%
Bus drivers	561	25 to 34%
Industrial truck & tractor operators	431	5 to 13%
Operating engineers	157	25 to 34%

Technical Support

Engineering technicians	755	24 to 34%
Licensed practical nurses	644	35% or more
Computer programmer	565	35% or more
Other health technicians	522	35% or more
Other technicians	346	24 to 35%
Drafters	258	5 to 13%
Medical technologists & technicians	246	14 to 24%
Science technicians		14 to 24%

Production

Misc. production workers	1,997	5 to 14%
Supervisors	1,800	5 to 13%
Metal & plastic-working machine ops.	1,473	–4 to 4%
Apparel workers	1,037	–5 or more
Inspectors, testers & graders	668	–4 to 4%
Welders, cutters & welding machine ops.	427	–4 to 4%
Machinists	386	5 to 13%
Butchers & meat cutters	355	–5% or more
Precision assemblers	352	–5% or more
Woodworkers	349	5 to 13%
Textile machinery operators	289	–5 or more
Printing press operators	251	14 to 24%
Electrical & electronic assemblers	232	–5% or more
Prepress workers	186	14 to 24%

	Jobs in Thousands 1990	Projected Growth 1990 to 2005
Laundry & drycleaning machine ops.	173	14 to 24%
Painting & Coating machine ops.	160	–4 to 4%

Repair and Installation

General maintenance mechanics	1,128	14 to 24%
Automotive mechanics	757	14 to 24%
Other mechanics	718	5 to 13%
Industrial machinery repairers	474	5 to 13%
Electronic equipment repairers	444	5 to 13%
Diesel mechanics	268	14 to 24%
Line installers & cable splicers	232	–5% or more
Automotive body repairers	219	14 to 24%
Heating, a/c, & refrigeration mechanics	219	14 to 24%

Unskilled Labor

Miscellaneous unskilled workers	2,082	5 to 13%
Freight, stock & material movers	881	5 to 13%
Packers & packagers	667	5 to 13%
Construction trades helpers	549	5 to 13%
Machine feeders & loaders	255	5 to 13%
Service station attendants	245	–5 or more
Vehicle & equipment cleaners	240	14 to 24%

Agriculture and Forestry

Farm operators & managers	1,223	–5% or more
Farm workers	837	–5% or more
Other farm & forestry workers	338	5 to 13%

Construction Trades

Carpenters	1,077	14 to 24%
Other trades & miners	863	N.A.
Electricians	548	25 to 34%
Painters & paperhangers	453	14 to 24%
Plumbers & pipefitters	379	14 to 24%
Bricklayers & stonemasons	152	14 to 24%
Highway maintenance workers	151	14 to 24%

	Jobs in Thousands 1990	Projected Growth 1990 to 2005
Administrative Support		
Record clerks	3,761	5 to 13%
Traffic, shipping & stock clerks	3,755	5 to 13%
Secretaries	3,576	14 to 24%
General office clerks	2,737	14 to 24%
Word processors & data-entry keyers	1,448	−4 to 24%
Information clerks	1,400	35% or more
Clerical supervisors & managers	1,218	14 to 24%
Adjusters, investigators & collectors	1,088	14 to 24%
Teacher aides	808	25 to 34%
Postal clerks & mail carriers	607	5 to 23%
Bank tellers	517	−5% or more
Other clerical workers	325	5 to 13%
Telephone operators	319	5 to 13%
Computer operators	280	5 to 13%
Mail clerks & authorizers	240	14 to 24%
Duplicating & office machine ops.	169	5 to 13%
Miscellaneous Service		
Food & beverage	4,400	25 to 34%
Chefs, cooks & kitchen workers	3,100	25 to 34%
Janitors & cleaners	3,000	14 to 24%
Nursing & psychiatric aides	1,374	35% or more
Preschool workers	990	35% or more
Guards	883	25 to 34%
Gardeners & groundskeepers	874	35% or more
Private-household workers	782	−5 or more
Other service workers	727	14 to 24%
Barbers & cosmetologists	713	14 to 24%
Police, detectives & special agents	665	14 to 24%
Home health & housekeeping aides	391	35% or more
Firefighters	280	14 to 24%
Correction officers	230	35% or more
Amusement & recreation attendants	184	14 to 24%
Dental assistants	176	25 to 34%
Medical assistants	165	35% or more

	Jobs in Thousands 1990	Projected Growth 1990 to 2005
Armed Forces		
Enlisted personnel	1,742	–5% or more
Officers	295	–5% or more

Index